M000095224

PLEASE,

Step into my Office

C. D. RENCHER

authorHOUSE®

AuthorHouse™
1663 Liberty Drive
Bloomington, IN 47403
www.authorhouse.com
Phone: 1-800-839-8640

© *2012 by C. D. Rencher. All rights reserved.*

No part of this book may be reproduced, stored in a retrieval system, or transmitted by any means without the written permission of the author.

Published by AuthorHouse   07/05/2012

ISBN: 978-1-4772-2964-4 (sc)
ISBN: 978-1-4772-2965-1 (e)

Library of Congress Control Number: 2012911337

Any people depicted in stock imagery provided by Thinkstock are models, and such images are being used for illustrative purposes only.
Certain stock imagery © Thinkstock.

This book is printed on acid-free paper.

Because of the dynamic nature of the Internet, any web addresses or links contained in this book may have changed since publication and may no longer be valid. The views expressed in this work are solely those of the author and do not necessarily reflect the views of the publisher, and the publisher hereby disclaims any responsibility for them.

In loving memory of Luvenia Barry, my grandmother
and my best friend. From day one she taught me
honesty, integrity, and the value of hard work.
I love you and miss you.
Thank you.

CONTENTS

Part 3
Gratuity

ACKNOWLEDGEMENTS

S pecial thanks to McArthur "Mr. Mac" Golliday and "Taco," two veteran bartenders who have forgotten more than most bartenders know about tending bar. They started off as my mentors. Under their tutelage I became their peer, and for always they will be the *best* friends a guy could hope to have.

Thank you, Reggie Bullock, a nice person who, on a slow Saturday afternoon, listened to a couple of my stories, liked what he heard, and encouraged me to write them down and put them in a book of my own. Without your inspiration and encouragement, this book would not exist. Once again, *thank you.*

Special thanks to Dan Roberts, a good friend, who sat and patiently listened to all my grandiose plans and get-rich schemes, never judgmental, always encouraging me to follow up on my dreams. Thank you, my friend.

Thank you, Martez Moody; you have been a great sounding board throughout the process of writing this book. I appreciate all your brutally honest feedback, while *always* encouraging me to continue writing. Thank you, sir.

INTRODUCTION

I will love the light because it shows me the way, yet I will endure the darkness because it shows me the stars.

—*Og Mandino*

I have been a bartender for the better part of sixteen years. As a young person, I never imagined that I would grow up to have a career tending bar. I dreamed of being a professional athlete, a firefighter, or an engineer. But bartending fell into my lap by accident, so I took it and ran with it.

Being a bartender has definitely enhanced my life. To this day I am thankful to have had this career. Working as a bartender has afforded me the opportunity to meet interesting people from all walks of life and from around the world. As a bartender, I have earned an above average income, from which I have been able to take care all of my personal needs, with more than a little left over to satisfy some of my extravagant wants. It hasn't always been a bed of roses, but for the most part, the good far outweighs the bad. And think about it: Who among us works at a perfect, utopian job? We all have to endure and persevere bad times at one time or another in order to truly appreciate the good times.

I have always enjoyed telling stories, whether about things that have happened to me personally, situations I have observed, or interesting tales that were shared with me by someone else. In Malcolm Gladwell's book *The Tipping Point*, I was introduced to the word *maven*, a Yiddish word for a person who accumulates knowledge and passes it on. I consider myself a maven. Being a bartender in a convention hotel in downtown St. Louis is a perfect job for a maven. The hotel bar is like an epicenter of knowledge, where people from all around the world and from all walks of life intermingle and share information about themselves, where they're from, and what they have experienced. It's an information bonanza.

On a slow Saturday day shift, I met a documentary film director named Reggie Bullock. He was in town to give a speech at a local church. Mr. Bullock kept me company on a slow shift. I made him a few margaritas, he had lunch, and we talked for a couple of hours. I was excited to meet a filmmaker because I'm a huge movie fan, and I've always been intrigued and interested in how movies are made. He talked about the film industry and told me about his documentary that he was in town to give a speech about. And I, in turn, shared some of my bar stories with him. To my surprise, he thought my stories were both interesting and entertaining. I considered this a huge compliment, and I was flattered, because I think that the people who make movies are the ultimate storytellers.

Then he knocked me for a loop when he suggested that I write a book about my experiences as a bartender that includes my bar stories. Initially, I didn't take him seriously because I thought he was just being kind. Who would want to read a book written by me? Sensing my reluctance to embrace his idea, he reassured me that he thought the few stories I had told him were good, and if I had more stories like them, he thought they could all be put together to form a good book. For the rest of his stay at the hotel, he made a point to stop by the bar every chance he got and persistently encouraged me to write my book. After he checked out and before he left, he sought me out and made me promise to at least consider the prospect. I said I would.

After that weekend, not a day went by when I didn't think about my book. For the next couple of years I worked on the stories and the structure only in my head, but over that time period I never wrote anything down. My procrastination was due entirely to fear: Fear that I couldn't write. Fear that if I did write the book, no one would publish it. Fear that if I did get it published, no one would want to buy it and read it. Fear that people wouldn't like it when they read it. My writing insecurity was based on the fact that when I was in school I hadn't done well in English. Also, I had never taken any writing classes.

The key breakthrough that inspired me to put pen to paper was a quote by Amanda Bell, which one of my friends posted on Facebook: "You can't teach creativity." I read that quote over and over again, all the while seeing the encouraging and supportive expression of Mr. Bullock's face in my mind when he made me promise to consider writing the book. Then I started talking to myself (my mother always said it's okay to talk to yourself as long as you don't answer), telling myself to try, and that I had nothing to lose and everything to gain. If I tried and gave it a 100 percent effort, how could it not be successful? And if I didn't believe in myself, who would?

Over the last couple of years I had envisioned this book as a collection of short stories sandwiched in the middle of a "how to bartend" book, but as I started to write, something unexpected poured out of my brain onto the pages, and I must admit it has been a pleasant surprise. I never imagined the self-awakening journey that writing this book has taken me on.

My primary goal is to show readers glimpses of other lives that exist simultaneously with their own, observed and retold from the point of view of *me*, their bartender. I hope everyone who reads this book will enjoy it.

PART 1

BARTENDING 101, MY POINT OF VIEW

JUST A JOB? OR A CAREER?

If you have a job you enjoy, you will never work a day in your life.
—*Confucius*

I have always loved to drink and party. When I was a young adult, I could work a twelve-hour shift, from 6:00 a.m. till 6:00 p.m., eat dinner, go out to the club, drink and party till 3:00 a.m., eat late-night breakfast, go back to work fifteen minutes before my shift started, take a nap for that fifteen minutes, work another twelve-hour shift, eat dinner, and then go out to the club and drink and party till 3:00 a.m. again—*no problem.* Those were the days. Now that I'm a man in my forties—*no way!*

During those party years, like most young people, I didn't have lots of money (I still don't), so I would go out and drink whatever that particular watering hole had on special, and believe me, I would drink anything that was cheap. The good thing that came of that was I got to learn firsthand what different alcohols, beers, and wines were. And what they tasted like. The bad news was how sick I would be the next day. I would sit across the bar and watch and learn how to make drinks (easy ones like rum and coke or vodka and orange juice), so when it came to applying for my first bartending job, I knew enough to bullshit my way through the interview and get the job. Once I was hired, I was lucky to work with Mac and Taco, two veteran mixologists who took me into their care and taught me a lot about bartending. Mac and Taco have since passed away. *Thank you for everything guys*. RIP.

I've been in the hospitality business for the better part of sixteen years. During that time span, at one time or another, I have held every position in a bar or restaurant. I've been a disc jockey, a doorman, a server, a cashier, a bar back, a bartender, and a manager. I've worked in adult clubs (strip clubs), bar and grille, and four-star hotels. Through hard work and diligence, I have fared well in most hospitality jobs, but when it comes to bartending I am a *natural*. Don't get me wrong: When I'm bartending I do work hard; it just feels effortless.

One of the keys to my success in tending bar is my ability to remember repeat customers and their drink of choice. In the eighties there was an American situation comedy television series called *Cheers*. The show was set in the Cheers bar (named for the toast "Cheers!") in Boston, Massachusetts, where a group of locals met to drink, relax, chat, and have fun. The theme song for the show was "Where Everybody Knows Your Name." Growing up, I loved that show, and as an adult working in the bar business, I now understand the meaning of that theme song. People do like to be remembered. When customers who haven't been to your establishment in months walk in, and before they even say a word, you greet them by name and put their favorite drinks down in front of them, it blows them away. I believe it makes them feel special. I can do that—not all the time for every customer, but more often than my average peer.

In *The Autobiography of Malcolm X* as told to Alex Haley, there was a numbers runner named West Indian Archie who Malcolm Little (Malcolm X) knew when he lived in Harlem. West Indian Archie had the kind of photographic memory that made him an elite numbers runner. He never wrote down the numbers people gave him, even in the case of combination plays. He was able to file all the numbers and bet amounts in his head and write them down for the banker (the person who organized and ran the illegal gaming). To me his photographic memory is an amazing gift. Later in life, Malcolm X wondered whether, if West Indian Archie had grown up in a positive, nurturing environment with his gift, he might have been a mathematical genius. The reason I mention West Indian Archie is that I believe everyone has a God-given unique ability that allows him to excel at some things better than others can. For me that ability is bartending.

> You are never too old to set another goal or to dream a new
> dream.
>
> —*C. S. Lewis*

A guest once asked me, "Where do you see yourself in five years?" Up until that moment, the question had never, ever crossed my mind. Until then I had lived life day-to-day. I didn't know what to say. I felt embarrassed, so I lied and told the man that I was in school, and that in five years I would graduate from college with a master's in business administration; then I would get a "real job." The guest commended me on going to school, and he encouraged me to stay the course and graduate. Then he suggested that if the opportunity to get a "real job" didn't pan out, I might want to consider a career as a bartender. He thought that I was really good at it, and he could see me being very successful. He pointed out that in most communities around the world; the bartender holds a prestigious and integral position in the community. He also pointed out that if you combine a bartender's hourly wage and his tips, a bartender's earnings are greater than most blue-collar jobs, and is comparable to some white-collar jobs.

This guest gave me a lot to think about. Before then, I never considered bartending as a career. To me bartending was something people do as a part-time job while they are in college, or to supplement their income while working a full-time job, but a career? I was in my late twenties, bartending was the only thing I had going for myself, and during that time of my life, I was sad, depressed, and felt embarrassed about where I was professionally. I was running out of options for a successful future, but this suggestion provided a glimmer of hope.

I was doing better than average as a bartender, but I wasn't even giving it an honest effort. What if I embraced bartending as viable career option and worked at it? I was making decent money. What if I learned more about different liquors, beers, and wines? Then I could make my customers better drinks and enhance their experience. I decided then and there that bartending would be my career, for better or worse. Since making that decision to immerse myself into bartending, I have learned much about the bar business. As a novice, I never imagined how complex bartending could be. It's way more than just opening beer, pouring wine, and making mixed drinks.

BARMAID

"Beauty has no obvious use; nor is there any clear cultural necessity for it. Yet civilization could not do without it.
–Sigmund Freud

S ome shifts at the bar can be slower than others, and then there are those very bleak, slow shifts when not even one person enters the bar. On one such day, an older gentleman entered the bar, walked around checking out the pictures on the wall, looked at the fixtures, and sat down briefly on various chairs in the establishment. After surveying the surroundings, he approached the bar. I walked over to him, welcomed him to the bar, and asked, "Would you be interested in dining with us today?"

He told me that he wasn't hungry and asked, "Is the bar open for drinks?"

I told him that we were open for drinks and asked, "What would you like?"

He started looking around as if he were looking for someone. After about ten seconds of awkward silence he said, "I'm fine and don't need anything right now."

I introduced myself and told him if he changed his mind not to hesitate to let me know, and I would take care of him right away.

He had a seat at the bar and started watching television. Every few minutes or so, he would look around as if he were still looking for someone. After about ten minutes he beckoned for me. I quickly went over to him and asked, "What can I get for you?"

He asked, "Are you the only person working at the bar today? Earlier you said 'dining with *us*,' and '*we* are open.' Where are the others at?"

I told him, "I am the only one working. When I said *we* and *us*, I meant the bar as a business, so I referred to myself in first person plural. If there is anything you need though, I can definitely make it for you."

He said, "I do want a drink, but I've never been served a drink by a man, and I'm not about to start now!"

I didn't say a word. There were a few more moments of awkward silence, and then he got up and walked out of the bar. That was strange.

Thirty minutes later he returned, started a tab with me, and had a few drinks. When he closed his tab, he left me personally zero money—no tip at all—and left. He must have really needed a drink but couldn't find anywhere else to go, so he acquiesced, returned, and allowed a man to serve him, but *darn it*, he was *not* gonna be forced to tip a man too. *Oh well!*

The encounter with that gentleman was an extreme-case scenario, but a true story and more common than most people would think. Very few bars employ male bartenders. My best guesstimate is that six out of every ten bartenders are women, and eight out of every ten food servers are women. Almost all US small businesses and companies are equal opportunity employers, but most bars and nightclubs will not even entertain the notion of hiring a male bartender; they prefer and hire only female bartenders. This practice constitutes blatant gender discrimination, but the discrimination goes one step further: the female bartender has to be attractive, too. I have applied for bartending jobs where the potential employer requested that a headshot photo be submitted with the application. You can't determine if someone is skilled, knowledgeable, honest, or a good worker by an applicant's looks, but if that employer doesn't think you are attractive, you won't even get an interview. My intent is not to imply that females who have a job tending bar cannot be good bartenders, or that their employment is based solely on their appearance. When I take a step back and look at the hiring practice of a lot of these bars from a strictly male point of view, I understand the method behind the madness. The vast majority of bar patrons are males, and having a pretty female bartender is an asset. I, like most of my peers, enjoy buying drinks and flirting with the "hot girl" bartender. My issue is with the employer who didn't even give the male or the woman he perceived to be not attractive an opportunity. I just bear witness to an accepted, biased culture of hiring that exists in the bar business, one that is unfair to both men and women. As I stand here on my soapbox, I proclaim unequivocally that any type of discrimination, no matter how big or small, is wrong and should not be tolerated.

At my very first bartending job, I worked Thursday day shift and Friday through Sunday nights. Friday and Saturday nights are the busiest shifts, so there were always two bartenders scheduled. Every weekend I worked with a young lady named Roxanne, a seasoned bartender who had five years of experience working in both high-volume nightclubs and mom-and-pop bars. She was a voluptuous young woman who had no apprehension when it came to wearing sexually explicit, scanty outfits to bartend in. During my "Roxanne era" of bartending, I made a huge amount in tips working with her. Roxanne and I had a successful formula when we bartended together: I would work the weak side of the bar and take care of the waitress orders and the female customers. Roxanne would take care of the rest of the bar, especially the male customers. We split any and all tips, and it was a financial windfall. I have to admit, the bulk of the money we made came from tips earned by Roxanne. The guys who came to the bar would give her obnoxious amounts of money. She would flirt with them, crack jokes with them, and drink and party with them. Some female customers (*haters*) had a lot of animosity for Roxanne, but she was a master diplomat; she would defuse their hate by killing them with kindness, complimenting them on their looks, their hair, or their attire. So the Roxanne era was the Golden Age of my bartending career.

To my dismay, all good things come to an end. Despite all of Roxanne's positive attributes, she also had a few undeniable faults. She was frequently tardy for work, she did not sell a lot of drinks (on some shifts, I would triple her sales), and she would get inebriated every weekend at work. (She loved to do shots, and customers loved to buy her shots and drink with her.) I personally did not mind her faults and did my best to pick up the slack and minimize the effects of her faults. Despite my efforts, after one year of working together, our boss became weary of Roxanne's shenanigans and fired her. I was angry, upset, and sad about Roxanne being fired, not just because of the money I knew I would not make because of her absence, but because she was a fun person to work with, and we had become friends. I mean no disrespect to Betty, Cathy, Donna, Julie, or any other bartender, man or woman, I have worked behind the bar with, but I have never enjoyed the elusive, unbelievable chemistry with any other coworker that I had with Roxanne.

Over the years, I would visit Roxanne wherever she happened to be working at. I would go in, have a few shots with her, and shoot the breeze. When I last saw her in the spring of 2008, she told me that her son had recently turned eighteen years old and he joined the Navy. Since he was grown and out of the house, she planned on retiring from bartending. She had saved quite a bit of money over her bartending career, and intended to go back to school and take some college courses. I haven't seen or heard from her since, but I truly hope that wherever she is and whatever she's doing, that she's happy and successful. Roxanne my friend, you deserve only the best.

I don't go out now anywhere near as much as I used to, and on the rare occasion that I do step out, I usually go early in the evening and frequent bars rather than nightclubs. When I'm out, I normally sit at the bar so I can check out what liquors that establishment carries. I take count of what liquors, beers, and wines they have or don't have in comparison to my workplace. I also take mental notes about the amount of alcohol missing in liquor bottles that I am not familiar with. I pay attention to such things in the hope that I can determine whether guests like or don't like that particular liquor and if we should consider carrying it or not carrying it at my bar. Another reason I sit at the bar is because I *love* observing my peers in the industry go about their business. My intent is not to steal any trade secrets; I just enjoy watching talented people do their thing, and to me watching a great bartender work is entertaining.

One of the most impressive bartenders I have ever seen was a young lady at a martini bar in the Central West End, an affluent neighborhood in St. Louis, Missouri. Playwright Tennessee Williams grew up in the neighborhood, and the house of the renowned poet T. S. Eliot is located in the Central West End. I would patronize this particular bar about three times a month. I consider the young lady who works there a *five-tool* bartender: she is a fast worker, she makes delicious drinks, she communicates well with the customers, she has an upbeat personality, and she is very attractive. I formed this opinion about her due to the service I received personally from her and from observing her make and sell drinks to other customers. During the shifts I have been there, she is always busy. Even if the other bartenders working with her were available, people would purposely go to her section of the bar and patiently wait their turn to be served by her. I'm not underestimating the fact that being extremely attractive played some part in her popularity; but even women, who at times can be a female bartender's worst critic, preferred her service to that of her male counterparts. Watching her tend bar was to me the equivalent to watching a baseball pitcher throw a perfect game, a master chef making an entrée at a five-star restaurant, or a quarterback marching his team down the field to score the winning touchdown during the last two minutes of a game. No matter how busy she got, she never became rattled, taking care of each wave of customers with efficient speed. I personally did not talk with her, other than her pleasantly taking my drink order with a smile, but I overheard some of the interaction she had with other guests. She possessed a vast knowledge of liquors and drink recipes, and she was very patient when it came to answering questions and enhancing customers experience during her watch. She is my bartending hero; every day I strive to achieve her level of skill.

MAKE IT RED

The more I know, the less I understand.

—*Don Henley*

What is rum? What selection of vodka do you carry? What's the difference between a chardonnay and a Riesling? Do you carry any IPAs (Indian Pale Ale)? A bartender makes and serves a wide range of alcoholic beverages. Depending where you work, you may sell beer, liquor, wine, or all of those. Having knowledge of the products available at your bar is a must.

I never personally attended a bartending school, but I hold such schools in high regard. If you have never bartended before, the instruction and training you receive from them is irreplaceable, and the possibility of job placement those schools provide could be a terrific launching pad for your bartending career. I can't help but wonder how much better a bartender I would be if I had started my bartending career off by attending a bartending school or academy.

A guest orders a margarita on the rocks. I ask, "Would you like salt on the rim?"

The guest answers, "Yes I would, thank you."

I salt the rim of a glass, then fill a mixing tin with ice, add a splash of sprite, an ounce and a half of tequila, an ounce of sweet and sour mix, a half ounce of lime juice, and a half ounce of triple sec. I shake it well, then pour the contents into the glass with the salted rim, and garnish the glass with a lime. The guest tastes it, and I ask, "How's your margarita?"

The guest responds, "It's good; I've never had one that tastes like this. What's your secret?"

I tell the guest (with tongue in cheek), "I'm happy you like it, but if I tell you my secret, I may have to kill you!"

I'm sure there are some people reading this who are saying to themselves, "That's not the right way to make a margarita." I'm sure a lot of my peers in the bartending business probably think the same thing. I believe the saying "perception is reality" is relative when it comes to making drinks. I have found that when it comes to alcoholic beverages, there are universal, regional, and personal names of drinks, ingredients in drinks, ways to mix drinks, and presentations of drinks. So if a guest asks for a drink that I'm not quite sure how to make, I have no qualms about asking the guest what goes in it.

A lady ordered a Tom Collins. I made the drink and presented it to her. She looked at the drink, then at me with a confused look on her face. I asked, "Is everything okay?"

She said, "Everything is fine," and paid me for the drink.

A few minutes passed and I noticed she had barely touched her drink. Fifteen minutes later I noticed that her glass was still pretty much full, so I approached her and told her that I had noticed that she had barely touched her drink and I was just checking to see if everything was okay. With a bit of hesitation she admitted that she was unhappy with her Tom Collins. I apologized and asked how I could fix the drink, or if I could make her a different drink.

She asked if I would mind adding some of the "red stuff" that she saw at the bar to her drink. Initially I was confused; what red stuff was she talking about? And then it dawned on me: grenadine. Grenadine is traditionally red syrup. It is used as an ingredient in cocktails, both for its flavor and to give a reddish-pink tinge to mixed drinks. So I made her a new Tom Collins, and this time I added grenadine to it. When she saw the new drink, she recognized what it was immediately. She took a sip and said, "Now *that's* a Tom Collins!"

This situation is an example of what I mean when I say "perception is reality." Now, most of my bartending peers along with a lot of other people would agree that grenadine is *not* one of the ingredients of a Tom Collins, but I always remind myself that my goal is to make my customers tasty drinks that they enjoy, not to preserve the sanctity of a pseudo drink name.

SHOT TIME!

During the spring and summer of 2011, one of the most popular songs in the bars and nightclubs in my metropolitan area was "Shots" by the pop duo LMFAO (Laughing My F★ckin' ★ss off). It's a party song that encourages people to drink shots of alcohol (usually an ounce to an ounce and a half), and it describes the fun that ensues. You could not go to any club without hearing that song at *least* three times a night.

The term *shots* actually originated during the nineteenth century, in the part of the USA that is sometimes referred to as the Wild West. Before we went to one currency, out on the frontier, people would sometimes use bullets for money; a guy would go into a bar and order an alcoholic drink and pay for it with a single bullet. Thus the term *shot* was born.

Rum and coke, vodka and cranberry, and gin and tonic are the most commonly requested mixed drinks. Bartenders usually serve those and numerous other mixed drinks as highballs in eight-ounce rocks glasses. A *highball* is the name for a family of mixed drinks that are composed of an alcohol-based spirit and a large portion of a non-alcoholic mixer. The bartender normally puts ice in the glass, pours the alcohol of choice (rum, gin, vodka, whiskey) in the glass, fills the glass with mixer (soda, juice, or water), and garnishes the drink with fruit (lime, lemon, orange slice). The standard *pour* (amount) of alcohol used to make a mixed drink is one ounce. If a customer requests a drink on the rocks with no mixer or neat (no mixer and no ice), the standard pour is an ounce and a half. Usually a customer is charged a one-dollar-or-more up charge (depending on the quality of the liquor being sold) when buying a drink on the rocks or neat. If a customer orders a double (twice the standard pour), the cost is two times the normal price of the preferred drink.

The number one most common complaint I receive from customers I have served mixed drinks to is about the amount of alcohol in their drinks (namely, the lack thereof). "My drink isn't strong enough!" "I can't even taste the alcohol in this drink!" "Are you sure you put the right amount of alcohol in this drink?" When faced with this complaint, the bartender has a couple of choices. He can pour another half ounce of alcohol in the guest's drink and charge him for a drink made on the rocks, or he could pour another full ounce into the drink and charge him double. Most customers choose the former, because it's cheaper.

The one thing a bartender does *not* want to do is give them more alcohol *free of charge*. Every day bars around the world fail and shut their doors. The number one reason is they give away alcohol. It could be the bartender, the manager, or the owner of the bar who is culpable when it comes to this self-destructive behavior. Alcohol, beer, and wine are products that bars buy at a wholesale price and turn around and resell to their customers at a retail price. *No* business can survive giving away its product *for free*.

Bartending is a self-policed job. The bartender has the responsibility to coworkers, to managers, and to the bar owners not to give away alcohol, or worse yet, to sell alcohol and keep the money, which is stealing. Keep in mind that if you give away alcohol or just keep the money, your venue suffers, and if your venue suffers and eventually fails and closes, then you, your coworkers, and the managers are all out of jobs.

So if you are a bartender, the next time a customer starts to browbeat you about the amount of alcohol in his drink, offer him the option of paying a little more money and getting it with a neat pour or a double pour. Another option is what I normally do: Suggest they buy an ounce on the side for themselves and their guests and do a toast. Shots! Shots! Shots!

BREAKING THE SHACKLES OF THE *N-WORD*

Time is the justice that measures all offenders.

—*William Shakespeare*

I HATE the word NIGGER! Dictionary.com *defines nigger* as "(4) slang: extremely disparaging and offensive, A. a black person, B. a member of any dark-skinned people, C. a person of any race or origin regarded as contemptible, inferior, ignorant, etc."

The word *nigger* is an artifact from a bad time in human history, one marked by slavery and later Jim Crow laws, when a cruel and inhumane thought process supported and allowed immoral injustice that included whippings, quartering, and lynching to be perpetrated on Americans of African descent.

My family taught me that *curse words* were bad and should not be spoken and that the word *nigger* is worse than a curse word. So as a child, if I said it, I would feel uneasy, because deep down I knew I was doing something wrong. If I heard it in a song or if one of my peers said it, I would feel uncomfortable, because I was taught to not participate and to stay away from negative situations and people who were doing bad things. If I heard a white person say the word NIGGER, it was worse than the sound of fingernails scratching on a blackboard. If a white person directed the word at me, more often than not it would elicit a violent response from me, because I would associate the word with its ugly history and the perpetrators of that history, the white people of that era, and the white people of the present (and wrongly so). I know now that for me and all other people of color to hold all white people past, present, and future accountable for the actions of a few is a broad generalization that is wrong, but there was a time in the not-so-distant past when I did not know better and did not want to know. Call me NIGGER and pay the price!

> You cannot serve people alcohol and get angry when they behave *badly*.
>
> —*Teddy Hustler*

It was a busy Saturday night, the club was packed, and the liquor was pouring. I was bartending with Cathy, my partner in crime, and we were clicking on all cylinders. Even though we were swamped, nobody had a long wait for service. Cathy and I were both in a great mood, we were making decent tips, and so far the night was going smoothly.

I approached the next customer. "What could I get for you tonight?"

He said, "I don't know, what you got?"

We were busy, and at a busy bar, if you aren't ready to order when a bartender comes to take your order, you get skipped. Sometimes you go figuratively to the back of the line, but I was in a good mood, so I told the guy, "Take your time, and when you decide what you want, let me know and I'll take care of you."

He appeared to be agitated by my response. I really didn't care, and started taking other drink orders. He started to yell: Bartender! Bartender!

I heard him, acknowledged him, and let him know that I would be with him in just a moment.

He waited a few seconds and started again to yell out: "Bartender! Bartender! What's a guy gotta do to get a drink in this place?"

I finished the drink order I had already taken, then I went to the guy. He was visibly pissed. I saw that, but was having a good night and I didn't want any problems. I said, "Sorry for your wait. What can I get for you"?

He was steaming, but ordered a Bud Light. I got his beer and told him, "That will be $4.50."

He started complaining about the price and was taking his time to pay me. My patience was running short, so I told him, "I don't set the prices. If you don't want to pay the price, give me the beer back!"

He continued to complain as he paid for the beer. I collected the money and started to take the next person's order. The angry guy turned to his friend and said, "That's why I hate NIGGERS!"

I heard him, Cathy heard him, and a few customers heard him. I went up to him and asked him, "What did you say?" He responded brashly, "You heard me. I hate NIGGERS!" I took my glasses off and told him, "When I'm done with you, you are gonna really hate NIGGERS!"

Cathy started yelling for the managers, and I jumped the bar to get at the guy. Before one punch was thrown, the bouncers broke the two of us up. He and I exchanged obscenities while being held apart. The managers got involved and told the guy he had to leave.

He said, "I'm not going anywhere until I finish this $4.50 beer."

He started to drink the rest of his beer, and while the bottle was up to his lips, I reached across the manager and tried to shove the bottle down his throat. Luckily for him and for me, I wasn't successful. Security escorted the angry guy out of the club and the managers walked me to the office. The managers told me that they understood why I was so upset, but that I could not attack a customer, no matter what.

I explained to them that when a white person calls me a NIGGER, that person is subconsciously asking me to whoop their ass, and that I am gonna give them what they want.

They told me that they sympathized with me, that they thought I was a good employee, and that they wanted me to continue working there, but any future behavior like I displayed that night could put my job in jeopardy. I would be better served to show some personal restraint.

Through clenched teeth and a fake expression of remorse, I said all the things I thought they wanted to hear. Then I returned to work and finished my shift.

> It takes courage to grow up and become who you really are.
> —*E. E. Cummings*

After work, at home in bed, I experienced a ride on an emotional roller coaster. First I was angry: angry with the angry guy for calling me a NIGGER, angry with the managers for what they said to me in the office, and most of all, angry with myself.

I couldn't sleep because I kept thinking about my actions that night. I could have killed that man. I asked myself, "Did the drunken guy—possibly not in his right mind—deserve to die just because he called me a Nigger?" No! I'm not trying to excuse what he said, but what if he happened to be a good guy who for the most part wasn't racist, was just drunk, angry, and lashing out, and the meanest thing he could think of at that moment to say was to call me a Nigger? Does he deserve to be badly injured or die? No!

Then I started to think about all the other times in my life that I went bat shit, Tasmanian devil, berserker, and ape shit crazy when a white person would call me a Nigger. As I lay there and sank deeper into thought, I asked myself, "Was it worth it?" No! "Was I happy with the way those situations turned out?" No! Yes, in the short term I had the satisfaction of retribution on my nemesis at the time, but looking at the big picture, did my actions really change anything? No! The only possible outcomes were: getting hurt physically; seriously hurting someone else; and maybe losing my freedom, going to jail for assault and battery.

Nigger is an *evil* word no matter who says it. So I asked myself, "What does that say about me? I had allowed the evil word *nigger* to enslave me. That word had become my evil master, and it made me do stupid and bad things. What an epiphany! That moment was a true turning point in my life. As I lay there, I started to cry. I cried because I was angry with myself for losing control so many times in the past and present. I cried because I felt embarrassed at the way I had been behaving. I cried because of the guilt I felt for possibly hurting someone. Deep down in my soul I knew that I was better than that. I know that I am a good person, and that I don't want to hurt anyone. I knew then that I had to be stronger and not allow not mere words, trivial things, to hurt me and become an excuse to behave badly.

I knew I had to set myself free from the control of the evil word *nigger*. I had to break the shackles that the word had on me. When I was a little boy, I was called fat (I was overweight) and four-eyes (I wore glasses). My peers teased me relentlessly, and every day I would go home in tears. My best friend then and always has been my grandmother. She would sit me down and tell me over and over again, "Sticks and stones may break your bones, but words can never hurt you." She would tell me to not let other people's opinions define me, and to stay true to my character. She said, "So what if they make fun of you and laugh at you? It's not really you they are laughing at. They're laughing at a stereotype: 'you're fat, you have four eyes.' A stereotype doesn't represent you or you it."

My grandmother felt that joy and laughter could cure anything, so she said, "The next time one of those kids makes fun of you and everybody starts to laugh, remember it's only personal when you allow it to be." She continued, "If you really want to mess with their heads, you should start laughing too, especially if what they have said is funny. Show them that the things they say don't bother you a bit, and as a matter of fact, you have a good sense of humor. Because sometimes it's better to laugh with people, than to be laughed at, as long as you remember: it's not personal."

> It's surprising how much memory is built around things unnoticed at the time.
> —*Barbara Kingsolver, Animal Dreams*

Thinking of those times and her words of wisdom was so apropos. So by letting those guys tease me when I was a kid, laughing with them, and learning that it wasn't personal, I developed tough skin and grew as a person. I started to think: it worked then; it would work now.

One problem: I wasn't too keen on hanging around people who used the word *nigger*. So after a lot of deliberation I decided that a more palatable solution would be to subject myself to *off-color* racial jokes. From that time until the present, I encouraged my friends to share *non-politically correct* jokes with me. Initially it wasn't easy. They loved me and didn't want to say anything that would hurt my feelings, but I kept assuring them that it was cool and I wouldn't get pissed. I must admit it hasn't always been easy for me either. There are some black jokes that are real stingers, jokes that if they were told in the wrong setting could ignite a small race riot. Some jokes are more social commentary and actually quite funny.

Breaking the shackles of the word *nigger* has been a journey, one that I am still on, and like most journeys, it has its ups and downs, but I know that if I persevere, someday I'll be the man my grandmother wanted me to be.

> If it walks like a duck, quacks like a duck, looks like a duck, it must be a duck.

In the past few years a new politically correct way of saying *nigger* has emerged: the term *the n-word* (the nigger word). To me there is no politically correct way of doing or saying something that is wrong. If it's wrong, there is no way to sugarcoat it; it's just plain wrong. Even though hearing the word *nigger* or the term *n-word* doesn't infuriate me like it used to do, nonetheless, when I hear them, I still become disappointed. It saddens me to think that a fringe group of people thinks it's okay for black people to say *nigger*, but if a white person says it, it's wrong. How hypocritical that is! One day I was Internet surfing and came across an episode of *The View*, where Whoopi Goldberg and Elisabeth Hasselbeck were discussing the subject of who can and can't say *nigger*. What sticks in my mind was when a truly emotional Mrs. Hasselbeck asked, "How do I explain to my children that the n-word is bad, when every day it's said by some black people and in hip-hop and rap songs?" I thought she had a poignant point. I guess I'm going to have to accept the reality that *nigger* and *the n-word* are not going anywhere. They are interwoven into American society, our language, and our culture.

The battle of the Alamo was a pivotal event in the Texas Revolution. One hundred Texans fought but eventually succumbed to the Mexican army. Their bravery inspired settlers in Texas to rise up and eventually defeat the Mexican Army. Their rally cry was, "Remember the Alamo!" I know I may never see it, but since the word *nigger* isn't going anywhere, wouldn't it be cool if it could evolve and someday become the rally cry for any and all people who are fighting cruelty, injustice, and evil in our world? I can imagine it now: Some evil dictator is being ousted by righteous people, and as the revolutionaries march into the capital to claim their victory, they are chanting as loud as they can: "Nigger! Nigger! Nigger!" Wouldn't that be poetic?

VODKA ON THE ROCKS, *POR FAVOR*

How terrible is wisdom when it brings no profit to the wise.
                                                    —*Sophocles*

I n the early nineties, for a brief time I worked as a certified nursing assistant at a hospital in Huntington Beach, California, in a general medical unit. The unit is a place for elderly patients who need medical care that can't be administered at a retirement home. During that time I had the opportunity to learn many lessons, not all about health care, which have benefited and enhanced my understanding on many aspects of people and life.

Daily we would have group therapy sessions where our patients would sit in a circle and share life experiences—not always good ones—with the staff and their peers. Our patients were all seniors, from all walks of life, who had come to the twilight years in their lives, when they need assistance taking care of themselves. In hopes of improving their health and their well-being, they find themselves living, sharing, and bonding with people in our nursing facility, whom under their previous circumstances, they would never have crossed paths with.

One patient in particular I recollect vividly is Mr. Dominquez, a Filipino man who spoke almost no English. The only thing I can remember him saying was a heartfelt, truly appreciative "Thank you" whenever you did anything for him. That wasn't very often though, because other than the nurses giving him his medication, someone from his family was always present to administer his care and take care of his every need. The love, attention, and patience that his family displayed while bathing him, feeding him, and doing anything and everything to make him comfortable, was a beautiful thing to observe. The level of care Mr. Dominquez received from his family was amazing not only to me, but to the rest of our staff and to our other patients. The other patients' families hardly ever visited and definitely never participated in their care. The other patients had no ill will toward Mr. Dominquez, but they did envy his relationship with his family.

Mr. Dominquez had a beautiful granddaughter who asked me daily for updates on his health and my opinion about when I thought he would be able to come home with them. During one of these inquiries I asked, "Why did her family come in every day and insist on doing all of his care?" She was quick to assure me that their presence there was not meant to slight or imply that our staff was not capable of taking care of her grandfather; they just loved him so much, and taking care of him was a privilege. I told her that I had never observed a family that was as involved as theirs was with a patient. She stated that she was sure it wasn't lack of love that prevented other families from being involved with their loved one's care. It was that what some people might consider extreme involvement was just their family's way.

She related to me a brief bio of Mr. Dominquez. He was the patriarch of their family, and had worked extremely hard his whole life to provide for them. Now that he was older and needed assistance taking care of himself, it was only natural that they would fill that need. She told me that the only reason he was even in our hospital was that he had gotten sick and needed to be under a doctor's care until he was well, and as soon as possible, they were taking him back home with them.

She went on to explain to me that for generations it was part of their family tradition to have their elders live with them. The older family members would babysit the children while the parents worked. Having the older family members as babysitters was a win–win for everybody. The elders got to spend quality time with the grandchildren and sometimes great-grandchildren whom they definitely cherish. The children were in the company of their forefathers and foremothers who possessed vast knowledge about life and their family history that could be passed down from generation to generation. If they were unable to babysit, as in Mr. Dominquez's case, the older people still deserved to be cared for and to have the opportunity to be present and watch their families grow. She was proud of the fact that he was an integral part of their family, and added that the knowledge and wisdom that they get from him and their other elders is beneficial and irreplaceable to them. She was aware that her family's traditions might not be right for every family, but it was definitely the right way for them.

After that conversation with Mr. Dominquez's granddaughter, I had a new perspective on how I viewed the elderly. As soon as I had an opportunity, I called my grandmother and told her how much I loved her and appreciated her and what she meant to our family. She told me that she loved me also and that she would appreciate it if next time I wrote her a letter instead of calling her collect. (That made me laugh!)

I have worked as a bartender off and on from 1996 till the present. On three different occasions I have taken a hiatus to try different jobs, always eventually returning to bartending, because it's the one thing that I am naturally good at. And it so happens that I make the most money bartending.

My most recent hiatus from bartending lasted from 2004 to 2008. I returned to bartending in 2008 when I got a job working at a downtown hotel, in its lobby bar. At that bar there was a hierarchy based on seniority. As the new hire, I was the lowest man on the totem pole. It didn't matter that I had worked as a bartender for many years and had lots of experience. Since I was the new guy, they always scheduled me for the slow shifts that my peers, who had seniority over me, didn't want. The shifts I worked had little customer traffic, so opportunities to make tips were scarce. Initially, this situation was very frustrating, so I started looking for a job somewhere else while continuing to work at the lobby bar.

One day, while working an extremely slow shift, out of nowhere, I had an epiphany: "When life gives you lemons, why not make lemonade?" I decided at that point to make the best of a bad situation. Since I didn't have a huge stream of customers to serve and make tips in quantity from, I needed to step up my level of hospitality and service to the few customers I did have. If I did, I might start earning quality tips. That realization was a huge turning point in my career as a bartender and in my life.

The day that I made that decision, I had only one customer all day: Al, a Greyhound bus driver. Greyhound is an intercity common carrier of passengers, serving over 3,700 destinations in the United States, Canada, and Mexico. Whenever I think about Greyhound, I can't help but hear the Supertramp song, "Take the Long Way Home." Al drove a route from Chicago to St. Louis. He would have a twelve-hour layover in St. Louis, then drive a bus route back to Chicago. During these layovers, Al would normally spend the night in our hotel. That's how I ended up having the honor and privilege of meeting him. After driving the bus most of the day, he would check into the hotel, go to his room, get settled in, and change clothes. Then he would come to the bar, read a newspaper, and have a late lunch. After he finished his meal, he would have an after-dinner drink: "Vodka on the rocks, *por favor*."

Al is in his late sixties, and was born and raised in Chicago. He grew up navigating the mean streets of that city, where he encountered, associated with, and was befriended by real gangsters. Not the *gangstas* you hear about in rap songs, but the type of gangsters they make movies like *The Godfather* and *Goodfellas*, and TV shows like *The Sopranos* about. Al emerged from this environment with a PhD in life.

Al had been a successful chef and a restaurant owner before becoming a bus driver for Greyhound. Al and I occasionally talked during his visits to the bar, and I found him to be extremely knowledgeable on an array of subjects: from music, to sports, the stock market, and a whole lot of other things. In some ways he was a walking, talking Wikipedia.

I was excited about my new "grand idea," and wanted to get Al's opinion on it. He listened patiently. After I finished telling him my plan, he paused for a moment, then told me he thought it was a great idea. He added that he felt that improving my level of service and hospitality would be beneficial no matter where I worked or how busy the bar was. He thought that I should always strive to earn *quality* tips rather *quantity* tips, and that the best way to earn quality tips is to give the guest *quality everything.*

I thought Al's comment made total sense, and feeling that Al could be a great source for more good insight, I told him I would appreciate any and all advice that he wanted to share with me, then and in the future. He told me that he thought I was a good kid, and that he would do anything he could to help me. At that time on, a well-received mentoring started.

I would see Al twice a week during his layovers. He would drink his usual beverage ("Vodka on the rocks, *por favor*") and tutor me on hospitality, service, professionalism, and what he considered most important: attention to details. He would listen as I told him about how I had been working harder to do a better job when it came to food service, making tastier drinks, and being friendlier to my guests.

He would commend me on my efforts, but he would always stress professionalism. He repeatedly told me how important it is to look and behave in a professional manner. I need always to wear neat, clean clothes, to make sure that my grooming and hygiene are impeccable, to speak clearly, and to be well-versed and fluent in information about the hotel, its policies, and the food and drinks that I serve. Al stressed giving attention to details: making sure that my workstation (the bar and the tables in the vicinity) is always clean; serving only food that is visually appealing (if I wouldn't eat it myself, don't serve it to my guest); taking ownership and ensuring that the food I serve is presented correctly (serve on the right side and clear from the left side); making sure that I make drinks that taste good and that are presented correctly (in the proper glass and with the right garnish). Al insisted that if I act professionally and pay attention to details, my actions will convey to my guests that they are welcome, that I want their patronage, that I understand and know what I am doing, and that they can count on me to do a good job. I listened, I learned, and I applied everything that Al told me, and very soon I could see a noticeable increase in my customers' satisfaction and an increase in tips.

Over the months that followed, Al's mentorship started to encompass more than just bartending, hospitality, and professionalism.

A dream that I have had for a long time and am still pursuing has been to own my own bar. I talked to Al about this often. He always encouraged me to work hard and never give up on my dream. Al had once owned a restaurant, so he knew what it took to be successful. I bounced many ideas off of him. Some of them he liked, but most of them he didn't. He reminded me of a Roman emperor in the Colosseum residing over my ideas, delivering the all-important thumb-up or thumb-down. Al and I had a brutally blunt way of communicating. If he didn't like one of my ideas, he would tell me so straightforwardly. His honesty would sometimes hurt my feelings, but deep down I knew that his intent was always to help me. As he would put it, "I'm gonna give it to you straight. I'm gonna tell you what you need to hear, not what you wanna hear."

I would talk to him about possible bar names, types of alcohol I wanted to carry, and types of food I wanted to serve. He would tell me my suggestions sounded well and dandy, but those things weren't what was most important when comes to owning and operating a successful bar and grill, restaurant, lounge, or whatever I wanted to call it. What's important is having a good location for a place that is clean and has a fun environment, where people can enjoy food and drinks that not only look good, but also taste good. It's important to have a staff that's courteous, friendly, knowledgeable, proficient, and that cares about doing a good job. He pointed out that the most successful companies have repeat customers, and if I want people to come back, my place needs to be consistent in every aspect of delivering a pleasurable experience to my customers. He referenced McDonald's: One of the big reasons it's so successful is that you can order a menu item from your local McDonald's, then go to any other McDonald's location in the whole wide world, order the same menu item, and more often than not that item will look and taste the same. That's consistency. Al admits that it's by no means easy, but if I can deliver a good, consistent product, in a clean, fun, hospitable environment, not only will my place be successful, but I will also make a ton of money. It was a lot to take in, but everything he said made sense. Al gave me some lofty standards, and every day I strive to achieve them.

In January 2011, I went to a local bar with a friend, where I saw one of the hottest women I have ever seen in my life. I sent her a drink via the bartender, and to my surprise she came over to where I was standing at the bar and thanked me for the drink. Not only was she beautiful, she also had an amazing personality, and she was extremely knowledgeable in something that is dear to my heart: health and fitness. We had a couple more drinks, talked some more, and from my point of view we were having a great time. We exchanged numbers, and to my surprise, she kissed me—and I'm not talking about a peck on the cheek either. (To this day, she remains the most attractive lady I have ever kissed.) The bar closed and we parted ways, promising to contact each other and hang out in the near future. Driving home I was on cloud nine, because it is so rare that I meet someone I am attracted to physically, intellectually, and socially who seems to feel the same way about me.

When I saw Al a couple of days later, I could not wait to share with him the details of my encounter with the young lady. Al listened patiently while I raved on and on about how beautiful she was, how smart she was, and how smitten I was with her. When I was finished, he asked, "Has she called you yet?" No. "Have you called her yet?" Not yet. Then he told me that I should not call her; I should wait for her to contact me first.

I asked, "Why should I do that?"

He explained that he understood that I really liked this braud and if she was everything that I described, most likely I was not the only one pursuing her. So the best way to distinguish myself from the rest of guys was to not do what everyone else who was chasing her was doing. "If she's interested she'll call you."

I totally disagreed with Al. I told him that if I didn't call, she was going to think I was not interested, and I would miss out on dating and connecting with a possible soul mate.

He said that there is no such thing as a soul mate, that he understood my reluctance to embrace his strategy, and that his intent was not to hurt my feelings. But if she felt the same as I did, she would contact me. If she didn't—her loss.

I told him that I did not agree with his strategy. Furthermore, I considered his approach the equivalent of playing games—pretending that I wasn't interested to gain her interest—and I didn't want to play games.

Al replied that he thought I was a smart young man and that naïvety did not suit me. He felt that life is a game where the happy people are the *winners* and the unhappy people are the *losers*, and the sooner I accept that reality and learn to play the game better than everyone around me, the closer I'll be to winning, aka *happiness*.

I listened to what Al had to say, but did not agree. I texted the lady that day, but she did not respond. I called her later on that night, but she did not answer, so I left a message. Two days later she still had not called back. I waited a week and called again, but again there was no answer, so I left another message. Until this very day she has not responded.

That situation was one of the few times I didn't take Al's advice. Was he right about life being a game, with winners (happy people) and losers (unhappy people)? To this day I don't know, but I hope that this is one subject he is wrong about.

How did sharing a simple idea and asking for advice turn into a mentorship that grew and evolved into a friendship with Al? I think that a combination of my subconscious need for guidance and the fact that Al was like a figurative cup, overflowing with knowledge and experience he didn't want to waste. In me, he saw a suitable receptacle for his invaluable wisdom. Did we always agree? No, but a friendship, marriage, or any other kind of relationship, if you always agree on everything, one of you is possibly being dishonest to the other, or worse yet, to himself. For better or for worse, Al and I were always straight up with each other. Whatever variables caused my friendship and later mentorship with Al, I have no doubt that I am a better bartender, and more importantly, a better person due to his caring tutelage. Thank you, my friend.

PART 2

PLEASE,
STEP INTO MY OFFICE

EVERYTHING TO EVERYONE

People come to the hotel bar to interact with other people. If
they wanted to be alone, they would have stayed in their rooms.
—*Meytal Ozeri*

For four-plus years, I have worked as a bartender in a hotel in
downtown St. Louis, Missouri. The building I work in was
completed in 1966. It was originally an apartment building, one of
three identical thirty-story buildings known as the Mansion House
Center. In 1974, the building was converted into a hotel. When you
walk into the hotel, the first thing you see is the front check-in desk. To
the left are six elevators, two of which are glass elevators. To the right
is an escalator that goes from the ground floor to the Promenade level
of the hotel. To the right of the escalator is a spacious three-story lobby
that was added to the hotel in 1999. The lobby is enclosed with stacked,
four-foot tall picture windows that start at the floor and go to the top of
the lobby. The lobby is decorated with comfortable couches and chairs,
available 24-7 for the leisure of guests. There are Dracaena marginatas
Bamboo palms, neanthe bella palms, Sansevieria, and Raphia palms
placed strategically throughout the lobby, all cared for by a horticulturist
contracted by the hotel. At the back of the lobby is the bar.

The bar is twenty-eight feet long, the top of the bar is marble, and
the base of the bar is covered with wood panel. The back bar has
a solid pine top, resting on a frame that has two open slots, where

two three-glass-door beer coolers rest. The back wall of the bar is a mural painting, a depiction of downtown St. Louis in the year 1848, from the point of view of the Illinois side of the Mississippi River. I consider the bar to be my "office," because it is the location where my duties are performed. If you read my job description, it says in short that my duties are to serve and sell alcoholic beverages. For this I am paid an hourly wage by the hotel, but I earn my living providing hospitality to hotel guests. Like most of my bartending peers, the bulk of my income comes from gratuities, and at my office, you are not making great tips if all you do is open beers and make rum and cokes. Depending on the establishment you work at, some bartenders earn their living by dispensing drinks by quantity, with limited interaction between them and their customers, but at my office, quality of service, not quantity makes you successful.

My friend Andrew defines *hotel guest* as anyone who enters the hotel. They don't have to occupy a guest room to be considered a guest. A guest could be a person attending a function in one of our banquet rooms, someone patronizing our outlets (the bar or the restaurant on the property), or just someone who walks in off the street to use our restroom facilities. It doesn't matter. As soon as he steps onto our property, he is our guest and should be treated as such. I personally consider hospitality as doing anything and everything that is within my power to make sure my guest has a satisfying experience during his visit.

Doug J. is a mentor and a good friend of mine. Doug has been in the hotel and restaurant business for over twenty years. On one occasion, while visiting Doug at the hotel he was the general manager of, a guest approached the two of us and asked, "Where can I purchase a Coke in this hotel?" Doug introduced himself and me as his friend, and asked the guest if he would wait one second with me. With a sense of urgency, Doug went to the hotel employee break room and using his own money, bought two cokes, and returned and gave the guest the sodas. The guest thanked him, and when he tried to pay Doug for the sodas, Doug would not accept the money. Doug told the guest, "If throughout your stay at our hotel, there is anything my staff or I can do for you, please do not hesitate to let us know."

Over the time I have known Doug, he has taught me many things that I will always be indebted to him for; but one lesson above all others stands out: "The customer is not always right, but he is always your guest."

When a guest steps into my office, I do my best to ensure his needs are met, whether that means mixing and serving him a drink, or serving him food from our menu. I do my best to answer any and all guest questions, whether information about our hotel, about the city, or directions to and from some destination. If I can't help, I'll connect him with someone who can. It's not easy, but I do my best to make an honest effort. I'm happy with my success, and I try to learn and grow from my mistakes.

A couple of years ago I read the book *Making Friends and Influencing People* by Dale Carnegie. One of the many things I learned from that book was the importance of a smile and a sincere, cordial greeting. A smile is so important when it comes to greeting people that the phone company back in the 1930s required their switchboard operators to smile when answering the phone. Always wanting to improve my hospitality skills, I am constantly tweaking the way I greet guests when they approach the bar, so now I make it a point to always smile when welcoming guests to the bar.

Saturdays are usually the best night to work when you work as a tipped employee in the bar business. At my hotel, the Saturday night shift for the bartender is 7:00 p.m. until 3:00 a.m. The beginning of the shift is normally slow, but as it gets later in the evening, business usually picks up. On an average Saturday, at the beginning of the night shift, I have a few people at the bar who were left over from the day shift, but otherwise it's pretty slow.

Once I was doing what I normally do: preparing to be busy, making sure the bar was clean, stocking beer, and making sure that I had all the popular liquors at arm's reach, when I noticed a couple standing in the lobby, staring inquisitively in the direction of me and the bar. I waved at them, whereupon they said a few words between themselves, and cautiously approached the bar.

Once they were at the bar, I welcomed them and invited them to have a seat. After they were seated, I offered them a food menu and asked if they would like a couple of cocktails. The lady, speaking for both of them, told me they had just returned from dinner, so they weren't interested in food, but they did want drinks. They just needed a few minutes to decide what they wanted. I told them no problem, to take their time, and when they were ready to order, to please let me know what they had decided on, and I would get it for them right away. So I went back to prepping, and every few minutes I would check back with them and see if they were ready to order something. They just sat there saying a few words between themselves while watching me work.

By the third time I asked if they were ready to order, they had decided to order a beer and a mixed drink. While I was making the mixed drink, the lady asked if I was the only bartender working that night. I told her that I was on my own, working solo. She told me that she and her husband were staying in the hotel all weekend, and that they were in town celebrating her fiftieth birthday. I wished her a happy birthday and asked if they were enjoying their stay at our hotel and in St. Louis. She told me that due to no fault of our hotel or the city of St. Louis, she wasn't having a good time, mainly because she was depressed about turning fifty. The only bright spot of her weekend was her visit to our bar Friday night and the bartender who worked that night.

She and her husband had just checked in on Friday night, so they put their things in their room and came to the bar for drinks and dinner. She told the bartender that they were in town celebrating her fiftieth birthday. He told her happy birthday, but did not believe that she was fifty. Bartenders are trained to ID everyone that looks under thirty years old; when she initially came into the bar, he debated whether he should check her driver's license. She told him that he was "full of s★★t." He should definitely be able to tell that she was over thirty years old. He adamantly denied her charges, and insisted that there was no way she looked fifty.

After some back and forth, he demanded to see her ID to resolve her disputed age. She gave him her driver's license. He inspected it and several times compared the picture on the ID to her. After a few moments he returned her ID. He told her that he accepts the fact that she is fifty, but in his humble opinion, she does not look fifty. She told him that he was kind, but she knows that she does look fifty, or worse yet, older. Angrily (but joking), he told them that if they intend to remain at the bar and for him to continue to serve them, they had to respect his opinion, and in his opinion, she didn't look anywhere near fifty! They knew he wasn't serious, but they relented and agreed. He smiled and made them a shot, and made them drink it, because as he put it, that day was a joyous occasion. "It's your birthday, and this is your first of many birthday shots!"

The couple ended up spending the whole night hanging out at the bar and partying with the bartender. They had a great time, all because of him. He's an awesome guy and a great bartender, so they came back that night hoping to see him again.

I told them, "It sounds like you guys had a blast Friday night. And I totally agree with you. I have known that bartender for quite some time. He is an awesome guy and a great bartender. Judging from what you guys have told me, he is for sure a tough act to follow, but I'll definitely do my best."

Right about that time the bar started to fill up, and I got quite busy. But no matter how busy I was, I made a point to make sure that the couple's drinks stayed full, and whenever possible, I engaged in small talk with them. Despite my best efforts, I could sense they were not having the same good time they had the night before. More and more people continued to come to the bar for drinks, and I did my best to accommodate everyone. After an hour or so the couple from Friday night asked for their check, paid their bill, and left, leaving me a one-dollar tip. I was so busy, I had no time to even form an opinion about why they left such a small gratuity. I just kept working hard, pumping out drinks as fast as I could.

The next day, when I was setting up the bar at the beginning of my shift, a server from the restaurant stopped by to chat before heading home at the end of her shift. She told me overall she had a good day, all her customers were nice people, and she made "so-so" tips. Then she told me about this couple she had, and how the lady pretty much "talked her ear off" about the bartender from Friday night. I told her I had the same couple Saturday night. The server said they were nice people, but horrible tippers. I told her about the one-dollar tip they left me after having multiple drinks at the bar. She told me not to take it personally; they left her barely much more than that. *Oh well!*

Later on that day, the bartender who was my relief was the same bartender from Friday night. When I started to tell him about the couple from the weekend who were looking for him, before I could even finish, he said he knew exactly who I was talking about. He definitely remembered them—the couple who were in town celebrating the lady's birthday.

He started telling me that when they first got to the bar, the lady was down in the dumps about turning fifty, but he did his best to cheer her up. I assured him that he succeeded, because all weekend she was telling anyone who would listen about how he was an awesome guy and a great bartender, and what a good time they had because of him.

He replied, "That's terrific. I'm happy that I made such a positive impression on them. They were really nice people. Their bill was two hundred dollars, and they gave me a one hundred dollar tip; they made my night. They were my only customers all night. Without them I wouldn't have made anything."

Before my co-worker told me how extremely generous this couple was to him, I assumed that they were simply cheap, but the reality was they tipped according to what their perception of hospitality rendered and a good experience at the bar was. I was disappointed that I didn't meet their needs and earn a better tip, but considering the circumstances of that night, I know in my heart that I did my best. For a long time in my personal, professional, and social life I have accepted the fact that I can't be everything to everyone. All I can do is give a 100 percent effort and hope for the best.

The lobby I work in has four-foot stacked glass windows on the street level facing one of the busiest metropolitan streets in St. Louis. Every so often, people walking down the street will peek in through the window, take a look into the lobby, and decide to come in, look around, and sometimes indulge in a beverage or food.

On a day shift that was no different than most of my day shifts, two older couples came in and had a seat at one of the tables in the lobby. I went over to their table, welcomed them to the bar, and asked if they were interested in taking a look at our menu and having lunch at the bar. One gentleman spoke for everyone at the table. He told me that they were staying at another downtown hotel, and they were out sightseeing before heading to a downtown restaurant they had reservations at that evening, so they just wanted drinks, no food. I told him that was cool. I took their drink order and got them their drinks.

They stuck around for an hour socializing, and they ended up having a couple of rounds of drinks. After their last round, they paid their tab and told me they were taking off when they finished their drinks. I thanked them for their patronage and invited them back anytime; I told them that if they needed anything else while they were still there, to please let me know. They thanked me for my service. I excused myself and left them alone.

When it's slow, after all my shift duties are complete, I stand at the end of the bar, surveying the lobby for new guests, and I watch television. It seemed like the four people at the table were talking and looking intensely in my direction. So I went over to their table to check and see if they needed something. One of the gentleman said they were fine, but if I had some time to spare, they wanted to ask me a question. I told him, "Sure, no problem. Shoot."

He asked me if I could name the last five vice-presidents of the United States. With no hesitation I named Dick Cheney (this happened prior to the 2008 election), Al Gore, Dan Quayle, George H. W. Bush, and Walter Mondale. The gentleman who asked the question slapped the table, and yelled at the other gentleman at the table, "Ha! I knew it! *Pay up!*"

I was confused; the other gentleman reluctantly reached in his pocket, pulled out a couple of fifty-dollar bills and gave it to the guy. I asked, "What was that all about?"

The gentleman who received the money told me they were talking politics at the table. His friend couldn't name the last five vice-presidents and he was giving him a hard time about it. The first gentleman said that the information is common knowledge—everybody knows that. He said his friend, feeling embarrassed, spouted back, "Not everybody knows that!"

He continued, "He started to survey the room, and as he looked around, saw you were the only one here, so he said, 'I bet the bartender can't name the last five vice-presidents.'"

The antagonist told him, "If you're so sure, put your money were your mouth is. I bet you a hundred bucks the bartender knows who they are."

Feeling cornered, the other gentleman agreed to the wager, and that's where I came in. The guy who lost asked me, "How did you know that?"

I told him, "I just love history. Between reading and the History Channel, I know a little American history."

He threw his hands up and said, "Just my luck, we would have a history lover here disguised as a bartender!" The guy who won thanked me for my time, and I went back to the bar.

Later on that night, I was hanging out with friends, having a couple of drinks, and I told them the story. Automatically, one of them screamed *racism*. "He thought you wouldn't know the answer 'cause you're *black!*"

Before I could respond, the other friend chimed in, "No, that's not it; he didn't think that you would know because you're 'just a bartender.'"

I told them that I think they are both wrong. I don't claim to know what truly lies in the hearts of men, but as far as I could tell, those guests seemed like nice people.

I told my friends that about fifteen minutes after I answered the vice-presidents question, the gentleman who won the bet came up to the bar, gave me a fifty-dollar handshake, and thanked me for my part in getting his friend's goat. I thanked him for his generosity, and took that opportunity to ask him how he knew that I would know the answer.

He told me he didn't know whether I knew the answer, but because of my attire, and because I was well-spoken, went about my job in such a professional manner, and seemed like a sharp kid, he shook the dice, and happily came up with sevens. I told him I was flattered and thanked him.

He took a seat at the bar next to me and told me he had something to share with me. Many years ago, he had a part time job bartending at a VFW (Veterans of Foreign Wars) hall. The tips weren't great, but he loved being around the old war vets who frequented the place. Those guys had been around the world and seen and done things he had never dreamed of. Listening to them, he became fluent in subject matters way beyond his imagination. It provided him with a crash course in history and life, taught by instructors who were knowledgeable because they had actually lived it, not read about it.

In time he came to realize that yes, he was the beneficiary of their vast breadth of knowledge, but he was also giving back to them. He was providing an attentive ear to people who needed someone to talk to. He told me that even though he does not know me, he likes me, and that if I was willing to listen, he wanted to impart some knowledge to me, as an old-timer who had walked in my bartender shoes.

He said bartending is a great job, and you can make more than a living at it if you understand a few simple things. Not to be undervalued is the importance of the ability to make drinks fast, and drinks that taste good. But the most important skill necessary to being a really successful bartender is the ability to be a good *listener*. He said, "You'll have all different types of people coming to your bar. The one common denominator that connects almost all of them is their quest for companionship. That pursuit may mean meeting friends, befriending people at the bar they don't know, or if worse comes to worst, they'll talk to *you*. So make yourself available, and by you doing so, both you and your guest will benefit. It's just something to consider."

Then he got up, told me it was nice to meet me, rejoined his friends, and they took off.

My friends just stared at me for a moment, until one of them said, "Boy, he was definitely wrong about you. Sharp? You are the dullest knife in the drawer!" Then they both started laughing, with friends like these guys, who needs enemies? Unlike my friends, though, I was listening to the gentleman; and sir, I want you to know: I heard you.

THE GEOLOGIST

You see things; and you say, "Why?" But I dream things that never were; and I say, "Why not?"

—*George Bernard Shaw*

I was born and raised in Illinois. (Go Fightin' Illini) The school district I attended held classes from the first Tuesday after Labor Day until the end of the first week of June of the next year. I didn't attend summer school, so during my elementary school years I spent June through August relaxing, playing with my friends, and watching television. One of my favorite TV shows was *Beverly Hillbillies*, a situation comedy about an oil company finding oil on this country bumpkin's land and paying him for the rights to drill for and sell his oil. The landowner becomes an instant multimillionaire and moves to Beverly Hills with his immediate family, where comical chaos ensues. I loved that show. To this day I can still remember a few lines from its theme music:

Come and listen to a story 'bout a man named Jed.
Poor mountaineer, barely kept his family fed.
Then one day he was shooting for some food,
And up through the ground come a-bubbling crude.
(Oil that is. Black gold, Texas tea.)
—The Ballad of Jed Clampett written by Paul Henning

When I was a little boy, I knew that we got gas for our car from oil—I didn't know how. Not until I was an adult and met a gentleman named Jerry did I truly begin to grasp why oil is called *black gold*.

One day, Jerry, a man in his fifties, spent a day at my hotel while on a cross-country road trip. Jerry was a very unassuming guy. You would have never known from just looking at him that he is an intelligent and worldly person. The day I met him he was wearing a plaid long sleeve shirt, faded blue jeans, and a generic brand of gym shoes.

Jerry was a geologist who worked for an oil company. He had been to Egypt, Saudi Arabia, Iraq, Venezuela, and many other places. Jerry was also a brilliant communicator, able to take extremely complicated information and convert it to laymen's terms that a novice could comprehend.

I told Jerry that he was the first geologist I had ever met and that I was a little embarrassed to admit it, but didn't know what exactly a geologist does.

He explained that geology is the study of solid earth, the rocks of which it is composed, and the process by which it evolves. He added that geology gives insight into the history of the earth, as it provides the primary evidence for plate tectonics, the evolutionary history of life, and past climates. A geologist is a scientist who studies the solid and liquid matter that constitutes the earth, as well as the processes and history that has shaped it.

Geologists assist in the exploration and discovery of crude oil, a naturally occurring flammable liquid that is found in geologic formations beneath the earth's surface. Geologists are also a constant presence on drilling sites, providing invaluable consultation throughout the drilling process, such as by helping choose where to drill. When an obstruction presents itself, the geologist on site identifies the type of rock that the company is drilling through and suggests a productive, safe way to precede.

Jerry sparked my interest, and I wanted to hear more. I had questions too. This day was one of the few shifts where I had only one customer all day, and I didn't mind one bit, so I refilled Jerry's soda and told him I wanted to get his opinion on a few subjects. He told me he would do his best to answer my questions, but he cautioned me to remember that his answers were just his opinion.

Me: Do you think that alternative energy sources, such as solar or wind, will ever catch on and someday replace oil?

Jerry: I personally am a huge fan of the development and use of alternative fuel sources, but for the foreseeable future, those alternative fuel sources can lessen our world's oil consumption on only a very small scale. Solar power isn't reliable. What happens on a day when the sun isn't shining, a day that's cloudy, or at night? The same goes for wind power. What happens on a calm day when the wind isn't blowing? The only way those two types of power sources can ever be utilized is when we invent a safe, reliable battery that can store solar and wind power that's collected, and we can access it when needed. Until that day comes, those power sources cannot be considered viable replacements for oil.

Me: Okay, that makes sense. So how do you feel about the push to build electric cars, and for people to drive them rather than gas or diesel cars?

Jerry: I feel that electric cars are a fad that will probably come and go. The electric car has a problem similar to that of solar and wind: no dependable battery that can hold a significant charge for a substantial amount of time. Right now, most electric cars can travel only about a hundred miles before the charge runs out and they switch back to being powered on gas. So until a durable, long-lasting, and rechargeable battery exists that can be mass-produced at an economical cost for the average consumer, the electric car is not feasible.

There is another option, but it would be extremely expensive. To accommodate a society that drives electric cars, a new infrastructure of electric charge stations, similar to gas stations, would have to be erected nationwide. That means we would need to build these stations every hundred miles or so, up and down every road, route, and interstate. In every city, town, and village we would have to incorporate a system of rechargers similar to the network of parking meters, so people could recharge their cars while they are parked. If our government decided to undertake such a monumental project it would be the first and most expensive of its kind. The good news is that such a project would solve unemployment, because it would take a tremendous amount of man power to build and maintain the systems on a federal, state, county, and city level. It would be more feasible to invest in the research and development of a more efficient internal combustion engine that emits fewer emissions.

Me: Does that mean we will always be dependent on oil for gas to power our vehicles?

Jerry: I'm not implying that, but what the average person doesn't quite grasp is that gasoline for our vehicles is only one of many things mankind utilizes oil for. We have been using oil for a long time. Asphalt, which is a sticky, black, and highly viscous liquid that is present in most petroleum oil, is used every day in modern construction and was used more than four thousand years ago in the construction of the walls and towers of Babylon. At oil refineries around the world, crude oil is processed and refined into many useful petroleum based products. Depending on the boiling point, crude oil can be distilled into jet fuel, gasoline, kerosene, and plastics.

Me: I never knew that oil provided our society with so many things. What will we do when it runs out?

Jerry: Runs out? What if I told you that there have been occasions when oil companies have revisited "dry wells," and to their amazement, there was new oil there? Believe it or not, that has happened. I'm not trying to insinuate that oil is infinite, but what I am saying is that we don't know to what degree oil is finite. I personally think that oil wells have a lot in common with water wells. A farmer can have a water well on his property and that well can supply water to that farm for generations and never go empty. How is that possible? It's possible because the source of that well's water is a huge reservoir deeper down in the ground. So why can't that also be the case when it comes to oil wells? Some wells may be supported by vast oil reservoirs that we simply don't have the equipment to reach. Of course, this is just a theory, but depending who you ask, a plausible one.

Me: I'm envious of all the great places you've had an opportunity to visit. I would like to visit Egypt and have a chance to see the Great Pyramid and the Sphinx, but I'm afraid to go because I heard that there is a lot of anti-American sentiment in the Middle East and that it's dangerous for Americans to visit Arab States.

Jerry: The Middle East has in no way cornered the market when it comes to anti-American sentiment. And I don't want to be the harbinger of bad news, but it's dangerous everywhere. You can be robbed, shot, or killed here in good ole Hometown, USA. Yes, there are dangerous places in the Middle East, but the whole region and all its people should not be stereotyped because of the actions of a few. It's unfortunate that every day on TV, radio, and on the Internet we have pundits relaying fact less information to a misinformed public, basically helping perpetuate negative, incorrect thoughts and images.

I have fond memories of my time living in the Middle East. While working in one of the Arab states, I was befriended by an Arab man who lives and works on a farm that is on land that has been in his family for over a thousand years. The farmer is a hard-working family man, and a devout Muslim. The gentleman is a thoughtful, kind person who harbors no ill will toward anyone. This Muslim farmer had never met or crossed paths with a Jewish person, and contrary to popular belief, he considers the Jewish people to be his long lost cousins, because both peoples are descendants of Abraham. The gentleman did not like or dislike Americans. I was the first American that he had ever communicated with. [Note: Jerry is fluent in Arabic.] He knew of America, but had no idea where it is, or anything about its history or its politics. It's not that he is oblivious to what's going on in the world; it's just that his major concerns are to be a good Muslim—which has nothing to do with hate or violence—also being a good husband and father, and taking care of his family and their land.

Jerry checked his watch and told me that he had to leave. He needed to head to his room and get freshened up before dinner. I thanked him for the very interesting things he shared with me and for keeping me company most of day. Before leaving, Jerry encouraged me to follow my dream and visit Egypt, saying: "It's a beautiful country, and you owe it to yourself."

"Black gold." Thanks, Jerry! Now I get it.

PARAMOUR

It's an easy-money occupation, a first-class psychiatry."
—*Morris Day and the Time*

T he hotel I work at is considered a convention hotel. So when
big chain stores, wholesalers of commodities or national
organizations have their conventions in our city, my hotel is pretty
busy. Convention season in my city is normally from March until
Labor Day. The rest of the year we're pretty slow except for our
business travelers.

Many different types of business travelers frequent the hotel. We have
salesman who are in town selling their goods to local companies, we
have business travelers whose companies are in other cities and they
have been outsourced locally to fill a contract, and we have business
travelers who reside in other cities, but their actual job is in my city.
Normally, our frequent business travelers will check in on Monday
and check out on Friday, go home for the weekend, and return the
following Monday. Our business travelers are a diverse group (both
men and woman, of all ages and professions) and for the most part,
they are some of the most professional, patient, courteous people I
have met.

One particular business traveler stood out from the rest. Her name
was Ashley, an extremely attractive lady, with a dynamic personality

and a great sense of humor. Unlike most business travelers, though, she would normally check in on Friday and check out Sunday or Monday morning. In the beginning I didn't know what Ashley's profession was, and frankly I didn't care. All I cared about was that she was beautiful, extremely kind, and one of the most generous people I have ever had.

On check-in day Ashley would always wear attire that I can best describe as conservative sexy. Later in the evening, when entertaining a business associate, her attire would switch to low-cut, high-hemline, formfitting, after-five dresses. Her business associates were always distinguished, well-dressed older men. They, too, were always very nice and extremely generous. Ashley would make sure of that.

I noticed that during each visit, Ashley seemed to have only one business associate that she would meet with the whole course of her stay, and sometimes, but not always, that business associate would stay in the same room as Ashley. The first time I noticed that Ashley and one of her business associates were in the same room, I assumed that they were also dating, but as her weekend visits to the hotel continued and became more frequent, I noticed that she would have different business associates who would share a room with her.

Of course, not understanding the nature of their business, it seemed to me that Ashley and her business associates never worked. They would check in on Friday, have a late lunch and a few drinks at the bar, retire to their room, reemerge that night, and head out for dinner and some nightlife. On Saturday, they would go shopping, do some sightseeing, or take any of many other daytime excursions. That night they would go out and party. On Sunday, Ashley's business associate would check out and leave. Sometimes she would check out too. On occasion she would hang out around the hotel, relax in her room, or hang out at the bar, then check out the next day. All of the bartenders loved Ashley, not just because she was attractive and generous, but also because she was a genuinely nice person.

On one occasion, after Ashley had checked out and left, the hotel front desk manager and I were having a conversation about the weekend that had just passed. During the course of that conversation I mentioned Ashley and how much the other bartenders and I liked her. At first he didn't know who I was referring to, but after I described her, he understood exactly who I was talking about. He also thought she was very nice and super-attractive, but he told me her name wasn't really Ashley. He told me that her name was really Lily, and that he too had noticed the different "business associates" each week. He told me that most of the time her room is in the business associate's name, and that she can't usually get a room key until they show up. That's why she hangs out at the bar so much.

He went on to tell me that one day he was bored, so out of pure curiosity, he googled Lily's name. He found out that she had been arrested more than once for prostitution. Was I shocked? Yes! Was I surprised? Actually, no I wasn't. All of a sudden, it all made sense: Ashley was a high-end prostitute and escort. To some people it may have been obvious, and I am not naïve—I have met a few prostitutes in my life, but none were as articulate, classy, and sophisticated as Ashley.

Did it change the way I looked at her, perceived her, or felt about her? Not one bit! I never cared before what she did for a living, and now that I knew she was a prostitute, it still didn't matter. The only thing that mattered was that she was a nice lady who was always considerate, friendly, and kind to me.

I begged the front desk manager to not tell anyone else about Ashley's line of work. He promised he wouldn't, because he agreed with my assessment of Ashley and didn't want to cause her any unnecessary problems.

I did my best never to let on that I knew Ashley's secret, but I must admit she had sparked my curiosity. To me she was a rare combination of a professional woman: Vivian Ward from the movie *Pretty Woman* and Chelsea from the movie *The Girlfriend Experience* rolled into one.

On one weekday night, close to closing time, Ashley showed up at the bar. She wasn't staying at the hotel. She had been out at a downtown bar and just stopped by to see if I was working. She was upset and needed someone to talk to. It was a slow night and there were no other guests at the bar. She ordered a drink, and then she started to cry. I did my best to console her. I asked, "What's wrong"?

She explained that she had been on a date with her boyfriend, they'd had a fight, and she left him at the other bar. She was upset and a little intoxicated and didn't know what to do, so she caught a taxi to my hotel, and she was hoping that we had a room available because she didn't want to go home. I contacted the front desk, and they quickly arranged a room for her; and because she was a frequent, good guest, they weren't going to charge her for it.

She sat at the bar while I finished my closing duties and told me about her night and about the argument she had with her boyfriend. He was a married man that she had been seeing for two years. She knew it was wrong, but she had justified it to herself because they really liked each other, and he was unhappy in his marriage and had promised her he was going to divorce his wife and they were going to be together. They were out on the town that night and having a great time until one of her "business associates" happened to show up at the bar they were at. The business associate was very discreet. He said, "Hello Ashley, how have you been? It's good to see you," and went on about his business. After he walked away, her boyfriend wanted to know how she knew that guy and why he thought her name was Ashley. She got confused and scared, so she tried to convince her boyfriend that the gentleman had mistaken her for someone else and that she had never met him before. To her dismay, her lie didn't work, and her boyfriend (the hypocrite) accused her of lying and probably cheating on him. They ended up having a big fight, and she left.

She had another drink and continued on about what nerve her boyfriend had to be mad and accuse her of cheating, when he was the one who was married. She went on to say that she loved her boyfriend, and the other guy was just a financial arrangement; the other guy pays big money for what her asshole boyfriend gets for free.

After Ashley's last statement, she paused and stared at me, followed by an awkward silence. She had made a mistake and told her secret, but not knowing that I already knew. She was embarrassed, ashamed, and afraid of what I would think. She got up, put a hundred dollar bill on the bar for her tab, walked out of the hotel, flagged a taxi, and left.

Ashley never stayed at my hotel again, but I did see her a few weeks after she disclosed her secret. She came in on a day shift in the middle of the week looking as amazing as ever. Before she could even sit down, I gave her a huge bear hug and told her that I had missed her and was happy to see her. She told me how she hadn't been around because she was afraid of what I may think of her after what she had blabbed last time she was here. She was also worried I had told the rest of the hotel staff, and therefore of the possibility that she might not be welcome anymore, and in the worst case scenario, that the police had been notified. I quickly assured her that I personally had no problem with her or what she chose to do for a living and that I would not tell her secret to anyone. Also, as far as I knew, no one at the hotel knew her secret. (The front desk manager who did know had quit a week prior.) I could tell that she believed me and that she was definitely relieved.

She had a drink, and we spent the rest of the day catching up, just like two old friends who hadn't seen each other in a while. She told me that her real name was Lily (I never let on that I already knew), and I disclosed to her that in a way, I too worked in the sex industry: I worked at strip clubs off and on for eighteen years, and for the last nine years I had worked as a DJ at a local strip club. (More to come on this subject in the upcoming book *Impromptu*.)

It turned out that we have a lot in common. Ashley told me she worked as a stripper all through college. After she graduated, she hung up her six-inch stilettos and got a "real" job in corporate America. She made decent money at her job, but it was barely enough to cover her needs, her wants, and to pay back student loans. She was struggling. Her best friend at the time introduced her to the business. She was appalled when her friend first broached the subject with her, but her friend appealed to her to let her explain what exactly she did before passing judgment.

Her best friend didn't consider herself a prostitute; she considered herself a *provider*, because she was much, much more than a prostitute.

Her rationale for the distinction was, yes, she had sex for money, but it was spread out over an extended length of time, with social outings and companionship mixed into every encounter, which she labeled *dates*. She considered the gentlemen that she provided sex and companionship to *clients* because of the amount of money they spent over multiple extended time periods that were scheduled similarly to business appointments. There were no pimps involved; there was no standing on street corner, and definitely no Craigslist. And she, as the provider, chose the clients, not the other way around. That's why it was much more than being "just" a prostitute.

The best friend invited Ashley to a discreet social gathering at a local lounge that was being sponsored by a "dating" website. It was an invite-only party, and pretty much everyone who was there were past, present, and future clients and providers. Once there, Ashley was pleasantly surprised to find out that most of the clients and future clients were distinguished gentlemen. After mingling and talking for a while, she found that most of them were nice guys whom, if she had met them in a different setting, she would have definitely given her number to and possibly dated.

At this party she met her first client, and her new career as a provider began. He was a nice gentleman in his sixties, whom years later, she still sees periodically, and she is proud to say he is one of her best friends.

When she first started as a provider, she tried in vain to keep her "real" job and maintain them both, but one of the most important qualities of a successful provider is availability. If the money is right, you have to be accessible to your clients at a moment's notice; trying to juggle another job just wasn't feasible. Ashley never told me her age or how long she had been a provider, and to be honest, none of that was really relevant to me anyway. I don't know how much she earned a year, but I figured it was in the low six-figure territory, and that's not even considering the intangibles: the expensive gifts, the travel, and the most important intangible of them all, the referrals. Ashley estimated that over half of her clients were referrals from other satisfied clients. The rest of her clients she met on an exclusive, discreet, members-access-only "dating" website, whose constituency consists of clients, possible clients, and providers. On this website, providers browse, interact (using instant messaging), and vet potential clients. Is it a perfect, safe way to meet potential clients? Not always, but Ashley has heard of very few bad incidents that involve a client met on this website.

The more I talked to Ashley, the more intrigued I became with the shadowy world of providers and their clients. Once, I asked Ashley, if most of her clients had so much going for themselves, why did they seek out the services of a provider? Why not go out the traditional way and meet a girl? Ashley explained that there are numerous reasons why clients employ the services of a provider. A lot of her clients are extremely busy working, and they don't have time to date the traditional way. Other clients are involved in bad personal relationships that are unfulfilling for one reason or another. Others are simply shy guys who are inept when it comes to pursuing and dating a girl.

Ashley told me about one client who had made a fortune in the computer software business. This guy had spent his teenage years and his early twenties in front of a computer, so he had no social skills. He was wealthy, but he was also very lonely. They met through a referral and instantly hit it off. They see each other at random times. On a whim, he'll contact her and pay her an obscene amount of money to drop everything and take off to some exotic location, where they have a blast partying. While on these jaunts, he lavishes her with expensive tokens of his affection. When they return home, he thanks her for a great time, and they amicably part ways until next time.

She has another client who is a CEO of a major American company. This guy works sixteen hours a day, six or seven days a week. She calls him the V-Rabbit, comparing his energy level to the rabbit in the Energizer bunny commercials. The V-Rabbit will set up an appointment with her at a hotel that is adjacent to his office building because it saves travel time for him. One of his mottos is "Time is money." She describes a date with him as: he shows up, and there is very little conversation, just strictly sex for at least two to three hours straight, nonstop. He'll just keep going and going and going. Unlike the bunny who credits his energy to an Energizer battery, she believes his source of longevity is "a little blue pill." After he's finished, he'll take a quick shower, thank her for the stress relief, and then it's back to work. Without a doubt, the V-Rabbit is the most physically taxing of all her clients.

Ashley also told me about a client she recently stopped seeing and cut all ties to: a married man who had been a client for a little over a year. He hadn't done anything necessarily wrong; it's just she couldn't handle the emotional baggage that he brought to the dates anymore. He was a nice guy who married his high school sweetheart. They had three kids and a nice home in a good neighborhood. To outsiders looking in, they had a Norman Rockwell life, but for him the reality was bleak. He was extremely unhappy. He truly loved his wife and kids, but deep down he has always known that he has never been *in love with* his wife. He married her because she was pregnant. They started off as friends, with the hope that they would eventually fall in love and make the marriage work, but as the years have gone by, they have actually grown further apart intellectually, socially, and sexually. He and his wife have not had sex in over ten years; he does not desire her, nor does she desire him. He is both alone and lonely in his own home.

Ashley's dates with him were emotionally and mentally taxing. She had to end the association because she dreaded the dates so much that she considered one date with him worse than ten dates back-to-back with the V-Rabbit. No amount of money was worth continuing to see him and ride his emotional roller coaster.

Late one night at the bar, I received a call from Ashley. I could tell that she was upset. She was just checking to see if I was working and wanted to know if it was okay for her to stop by. I told her of course and asked if she needed me to send a taxi for her. She told me it wasn't necessary; she was en route and would be here soon.

She arrived about fifteen minutes later. She came running up and jumped into my arms. She was crying and hysterical. I helped her to a bar stool and got her a cup of coffee. After she calmed down, she told me why she was so upset. She was out with her boyfriend, and she told him that she was sick of being the "other woman." No more excuses—she gave him an ultimatum: Leave his wife and commit to her, or they couldn't see each other anymore.

They got into a huge fight. He called her a whore and said that he wasn't leaving his wife, and that if he did, it definitely wouldn't happen so he could be with her. He told her that she was delusional. How could anyone be in a committed relationship with a whore? That doesn't make any sense. He told her that however she tries to spin it, her job is being a whore, and she is not monogamous; so how could she ask her partner to be monogamous? He reiterated: that doesn't make any sense!

She told him she wasn't a whore, she was a provider, and she would quit for him. He told her he didn't care what fancy terms she used to ease her conscience; if you accept money for sex, you are a whore!

She had came clean and told him what she did for a living over six months ago. She asked him if he felt this way, why did he continue to see her. He smugly told her that it was a boost to his ego that he got for free what those other schmucks were paying top dollar for.

At that point, she stood up, punched him as hard as she could in his face, and walked away from him forever.

I told her bravo for hitting him and walking away, that I thought that he was wrong, and she was better off without him. She thanked me for my kind words and for listening and being such a good friend, but she felt a lot of what he said was true. That's why it hurt so much. She was a whore; no matter how she tried to clean it up, sanitize it, and call it a different name, at the end of the day, what she did was prostitution. She told me that as a little girl she never dreamed of growing up and becoming a prostitute. She dreamed of being a fashion designer and creating clothes that tall, beautiful, statuesque women would wear while walking down the runway in places like New York or Paris. But somewhere along the way to that dream, she got distracted, then she got lost, and then she became lazy.

I told Ashley that I thought she was being too hard on herself. She told me that, to the contrary, she hadn't been hard enough on herself. In college, when things got tough, instead of bearing down and persevering, she chose to be a stripper, a morally ambiguous way to make money. Now as an adult, she repeated the same mistake, but way worse by becoming a prostitute. She felt that she had sold herself out countless times; but she felt that it wasn't too late to stop this detrimental trend, and that she needed to reevaluate her life and make some changes. She thanked me again for listening and for being a good friend, and she gave me a hug and left.

After that night, I never saw Ashley again, but Lily did visit me a few months later. When Lily stopped by the bar, I was so happy to see her, I offered her a cocktail, and she humbly declined and asked for a soda. I told her how much I missed her, and that since I hadn't seen or heard from her in a while, I was worried about her. She told me she never wanted to worry me, and that she had been doing well.

Lily attributed her absence to the fact that she had been extremely busy. She had gotten a "real" job, and for the most part she had stopped working as a provider. She wasn't a member of the provider and client website anymore, she wasn't seeing any new clients, and she was seeing only a few "special" clients whom she considered friends. She had also enrolled in a fashion design school. I told her I was proud of her and asked if she was happy. She said like most people, she has her good and her bad days, but she definitely was having more good ones. She was healthier spiritually, emotionally, and physically, and she was optimistic about the new direction her life was headed. She added, "Life is tough, but guess what: So am I!"

Bravo, Lily, bravo!

ABSOLUTION

Judge not, and you will not be judged; condemn not and you will not be condemned; forgive, and you will be forgiven.

—*Luke 6:37*

I hate shopping! I will do anything to avoid it. I attribute my disdain for shopping to the fact that when I was a little boy, the adult women in my life (my mother, grandmother, and aunts) always dragged me along when they went to the grocery store, the mall, or a department store. They knew I hated going with them, when I would rather have stayed home and watched cartoons on TV or gone to the playground. They didn't care; I guess they needed somebody to carry their bags.

During one excursion to a department store with my great-aunt, she came across an Elvis Presley *Greatest Hits* cassette. She picked it up and started reading aloud the names of the songs that were on the cassette. She commented that she knew and liked most of the songs, and asked me if I thought she should purchase it. I told her that I hated Elvis Presley, and if I were her, I wouldn't buy it. She was taken aback by my response and told me that hate is a strong word; she asked why I felt that way about Elvis Presley. I told her it was because he had said, "All a black person can do for me is shine my shoes and buy my records."

She replied, "That's a horrible thing to say! Did you see him say that during an interview on television?"

"No."

"Okay, did you read an article where he was interviewed and made that statement?"

"No."

She said, "Baby how do you know he really did say that?"

"Well that's what I *heard* he said."

For a moment, she looked disappointed in me. Then she smiled and said, "Let's go get a soda in the store cafeteria." She bought us sodas, and we sat down because she had a few things she wanted to discuss with me. (She talked and I listened.)

She started off by explaining that hate is an extreme dislike or antipathy, and that no one should ever say he hates another human being. She wanted me to understand that we are all God's children, and that none of us are perfect. That's why scripture teaches us if we hate anything, to hate the sin, not the sinner.

Next, she impressed upon me how important it is to have as much factual information as possible before drawing conclusions about something.

Finally, she wanted me to understand that we as human beings should never try to judge another person. Only God can judge, because only God truly knows what lies in the heart of man.

We finished our sodas, and as we left the cafeteria she asked, "So should I get this cassette?"

I replied, "No. Let's see if they have a cassette by that guy who sings 'Jailhouse Rock.' I love that song."

She shook her head, laughed, gave me a big hug, and said, "What am I gonna do with you?"

I must admit, most of the things my great-aunt tried to teach me that day were above my head at the time, but I never forgot what she shared with me. As an adult, I always make a concerted effort to implement the knowledge she bestowed upon me, living every day in awe of what this world and its people have to offer an open, non-judgmental mind.

> Only God can judge me.
>
> —*Tupac Shakur*

On slow shifts at the bar, when customers are few and far between and all my side work is complete, I pass the time by watching the Cable News Network on television. I prefer CNN to the other news networks because in my opinion their programming is not left wing or right wing. They do a good job of staying in the middle, just giving their viewers the facts, which allows viewers to form their own opinions on social and current events.

On one of these slow shifts, one of the few customers I had was a guest named Craig. Craig would come to the bar and get a beer to take back to his room; this happened, a couple of times that day. The next day, he was at the bar when I walked through the door. This time he had a beer and also ate lunch. The interaction between Craig and me started off as just small talk exchanged during lunch that day. Over the course of his stay at the hotel, that small talk evolved into jovial banter about sports and girls, which grew to deep conversations about social and current events that we watched unfold on television.

My initial impression of Craig was that he had a glass-half-empty kind of outlook about most things. I in turn would try to present to him more positive alternative outlooks on the same subject matters, but not attempting to prove him wrong. I just hoped to open his mind up to possibilities other than always the negatives.

Over the course of time, and a lot of beers consumed by Craig, his level of comfort with me reached a level where Craig started volunteering unsolicited information about his personal life.

Craig was in his mid–thirties. He told me that he had spent a third of his life incarcerated, but he was in the process of changing his life. He and his family owned a lucrative tree trimming company. He talked about owning multiple expensive cars, having lots of expensive jewelry, and wearing custom made, expensive clothes. Up until recently, he lived in a bad neighborhood, and his jealous, uninformed neighbors were wrongly under the impression that he and his family were drug dealers. Recently, some dangerous people broke into his house in hopes of obtaining drugs, money, or guns. He was staying in our hotel until he could find somewhere else to live. To this day, I don't know what Craig actually did for a living. He was knowledgeable about drugs and the drug game, and he was also fluent in information about tree trimming. So he could have been employed doing either thing or both.

After that exchange, a couple of days went by before I saw Craig again. When I did see him next, to his amazement, before he got to the bar and sat down, I had already opened his favorite beer and had it ready for him. He told me he hadn't been around because he had been out looking for a new place to live. Craig hung out most of that day, had more than a few beers, and told me about his house hunting.

That day on CNN there was a story about Michael Vick getting picked up by the Philadelphia Eagles. Michael Vick had recently been released from jail after serving time for operating a dog fighting ring. There were people protesting and threatening to boycott Eagles games in response to their signing him. I told Craig that I thought that was messed up; Vick has paid his debt to society, and he deserves an opportunity to obtain gainful employment and have a second chance. Craig asked whether I believe that even a guy who was convicted of killing dogs for sport deserved to be forgiven and given a second chance. What Michael Vick did was heinous, and I definitely don't condone what he did. But he went to jail, paid his debt to society, and was released. We as a society have to believe in our legal system and the rehabilitation of people convicted of crimes. If we are not willing to give them a second chance, why let them out of jail? Craig just looked at me, smiled and said he had never looked at it that way.

Later that day, we saw a story about a child molester case on TV. To my surprise, Craig was very knowledgeable about the overall process regarding the convicting, sentencing, and parole parameters for a convicted child molester. I asked him whether he saw this story unfold on an earlier show. He said no; but his last stint in jail was due to a bogus child molestation charge.

"A bogus child molestation charge, what does that mean?" I asked.

Craig ordered two beers and a double shot of cognac. He did the double shot in one gulp, chased it with one of the beers, and started to explain what he meant by "bogus" charges.

His story began with his last serious relationship. He and his lady friend lived together with their children from previous relationships. In the beginning, they were all very happy. They loved each other, and their kids got along like brothers and sisters. They were, in his words, "a Hood Brady Bunch."

Sad to say, the relationship soured, and the eventual breakup was ugly. A year after the breakup, Craig, his lady friend, and her family were bitter enemies, but their twelve-year-old daughters remained close friends. He had no problem with the girls being friends until he heard a rumor that his ex-girlfriend's daughter was a prostitute. When he arrived home that evening, the two girls were at his place. He told them what he had heard. He did not want his daughter hanging out with his ex-girlfriend's daughter anymore, and she needed to get out of his house.

The girl said that the rumor was not true. Her mother had also heard the rumor, and before the girl could explain, her mother kicked her out and she had nowhere to go. Craig told her he didn't know what to believe. All he knew was she couldn't stay at his place. The two girls begged and pleaded with him to change his mind, and only because he loved his daughter and did not like seeing her cry, he agreed to let her friend spend the night, but he was very clear that in the morning she had to go.

He went out that night and partied with some friends. Later, back home, drunk on alcohol and f★cked up on marijuana, Craig lay naked in his bed about to pass out, when his ex-girlfriend's twelve-year-old daughter entered his room, and by his account, seduced him. He claimed to not remember exactly what happened, but he knows that he did have sex with her. The rest is a blur. When he woke up the next morning, he confronted the girl about what happened the night before. She acknowledged what happened, and hoped that he would reconsider and let her stay. Craig was incensed. He told her to stay away from him and his daughter, and forcibly kicked the girl out of his house.

A few days later, the police came to his house in the early morning hours and arrested him for raping a child. At first he denied it totally. Then he told them that she was a prostitute, and that she had sex with him while he was incapacitated, without his knowledge or consent.

No matter what he said they did not believe him. He spent a year in county lockup before they offered him a deal: confess to child molestation charges, and they would let him out with time served. Not truly understanding what restrictions come with being a convicted sex offender, and wanting to get out of jail, he agreed.

I stood there and listened, but was at a loss for words; I was numb. Craig started a rant about how he felt like it was all a setup, how his ex sent her daughter over there just to get even with him for some sh★t that went down between them. I just listened. I was in *shock! Shock* that he had sex with a twelve-year-old girl. *Shock* that he was actually trying to justify it and place the blame on someone else. *Shock* that he was even telling me this horrible story.

I didn't say a word, but I believe Craig picked up on my feelings about what he had told me by my lack of response, maybe from my body language, or maybe by my facial expression that I couldn't control, that I am sure was one of repulsion. He finished his beer, slammed it down on the bar, and walked away.

I never saw Craig again. I often ask myself: "Why did he share that with me?" I think that deep down Craig knew that what he did was wrong, but he was desperately looking for somebody, anybody to listen to his side of the story in hopes of garnering understanding. I believe he was seeking absolution in the wrong place from the wrong person. Because of my stance on many subjects and people, he thought that I would understand and sympathize with his plight. He was wrong. Yes, I want Michael Vick to be forgiven and given a second chance, but his crime was against dogs. I love animals and think they should be protected, but I'll always, always value human beings' (especially children's) well-being above anything else. Till this day I cannot rationalize, understand, or forgive what Craig did. If I were to run into Craig today I would encourage him to seek absolution through prayer, because I believe what he seeks can only be achieved through God's grace.

MY FRIEND

There is little difference in people, but that little difference makes a big difference. The little difference is attitude. The big difference is whether it is positive or negative.

—*W. Clement Stone*

The winter of 2010 was one of the worst winters on record for the United States. We had record snowfall for the East Coast and Midwest parts of our country. Here in St. Louis, we did not have as much snow as places like Iowa, Philadelphia, and Washington, DC, but we did have more than our fair share of snow and bitterly cold temperatures. Because of the bad weather, a lot of downtown workers found it hard getting back and forth to work. Many downtown companies footed the bill and lodged a skeleton crew of employees in downtown hotels, just to insure they would have an adequate staff to be able to conduct business. This turn of events provided a boost in revenue for downtown hotels, which normally are virtually vacant during the winter months.

At my hotel, the extra business was appreciated, but we did have some logistical problems. Our hotel staff was not exempt from transportation problems getting to and from work. A lot of my coworkers could not make it in to work, so because I live downtown and drive a truck, I picked up as many shifts as possible, working for people who could not come in. The extenuating circumstances of that winter ended up being advantages to me. I needed the hours; even though business is slow during that time of year, my electric bill, and car and mortgage payments *don't stop*, and still need to be paid.

That year, Christmas Eve fell on Friday and Christmas Day on Saturday, so a lot of companies who had sequestered staff at our hotel gave those people that Thursday through Monday off. So that weekend at the hotel, occupancy more closely resembled our normal winter hotel volume. I believe we had less than fifty people total staying in the hotel, a hotel that has 440 guest rooms.

One of the fifty guests was a gentleman named Petar, a jet pilot who works for a commercial company that supplies twin-engine jet planes for business and pleasure transportation. He was in town to test-fly a plane his company was considering purchasing. Due to some unforeseen issues, the plane wasn't ready for him to evaluate, and wouldn't be ready until Monday, so he was stuck at our hotel in St. Louis over the Christmas weekend.

Petar was originally from Bosnia, but he now lives in Zurich, Switzerland. Before Yugoslavia broke up into Croatia, the Republika Srpska, Macedonia, and Slovenia, he served ten years as a fighter pilot in the Yugoslavian Air Force.

I told Petar how much I loved history, and that even though Eastern European history intrigued me, I knew little of it, especially Yugoslavian history. Petar related his experiences, addressing me repeatedly as "my friend."

"My friend, my country has been known as Yugoslavia from 1943-92. Before that, it was known as the Kingdom of Yugoslavia, aka the Kingdom of Serbs, Croats, and Slovenes. For most of my life, Yugoslavia had been ruled by Josip Tito.

"My friend, Yugoslavia has a long and divisive history based on politics and religion, which I do not personally adhere to, mainly because of the time I spent in the military when I was in my twenties. My friend, I am aware of the dislike that existed between the newly-formed independent countries, but I personally do not take sides. My friend, to me *all* Yugoslavians—let them be Croats or Serbs, Muslims or Christians—are and will always be my brothers and sisters.

"My friend, after the breakup of Yugoslavia, I got out of the military and have since worked as a pilot for a few private companies. My friend, since entering the private sector, I have had the pleasure to meet and fly celebrities, captains of industry, sheikhs, world leaders, and the ultra-wealthy all around the world."

Petar never gave any names, but he did tell me some interesting stories that occurred during the multitude of jaunts he has flown.

"My friend let me tell you about my first job after I got of the military. I went to work for an Arab prince; I called him 'the Sultan.' He owned his own personal G6 Gulfstream jet, which he employed me to fly. The Sultan staffed the plane with eight to ten 'high end' call girls, whom he procured from all around the world. They would *party* to and from exotic locales all over the Mediterranean. No expense would be spared; the plane would we be stocked with the finest foods, champagnes, and illegal drugs. The Sultan would tip me handsomely on top of my salary for my discretion and my silence.

"My friend, I really enjoyed working for the Sultan. He was a fair man who was extremely generous to me. The 'flight crew' that the Sultan contracted out was made up of super-hot young ladies, but my friend, I never messed around with any of them. The Sultan had one unbreakable rule: *Don't f*ck with his b*tches!* Not to say there weren't opportunities, my friend. But why risk it and ruin a good thing?"

Petar's next story was about a celebrity he would fly down to Rio de Janeiro, Brazil.

"My friend, I would fly this guy down to Rio, where he would employ young male prostitutes, at least two or three at a time. My friend, I would fly them around for hours while they partied and did their business in the cabin. My friend, I could care less about whatever they were doing, to each his own, my friend. Straight or gay, I don't judge, my friend. I believe that it takes all types to make the world go round."

That Thursday shift went by so fast! Petar was an interesting guy, someone I enjoyed hanging out with and serving. On top of that, he was an extremely generous tipper. When my shift ended, I thanked him for everything and told him I hoped to meet him again.

The next day was Christmas Eve, and despite my best efforts, I was in a *shitty* mood. My grandmother passed away in October 1998, and since she has been gone, holidays are really rough on me. My grandmother, whom I loved dearly, was an awesome lady. She was my mentor, my best friend, and the one person who I know for a fact loved me unconditionally. I always miss her, but during the holidays, her absence is emotionally crippling to me. Because I'm so sad on holidays, I always consider just requesting off on those days, but I fear that being home alone, my depression would sink into a dark place that I am afraid I would have a hard time returning from. So I usually start my holiday day off with prayer, then put my best face on, head to work, and hope for the best.

An hour into my shift, Petar came to the bar for lunch. "Hello, my friend, how are you this fine day?" He was in a great mood and ready to hang out with me, his new friend.

Despite my best effort to mask my sadness, he could tell I was in a solemn mood, and he asked, "My friend, what is wrong?"

I told him nothing was wrong, and got him a menu and a beer. He knew I wasn't being honest with him; he could definitely sense there was something wrong. Over the next hour, he gingerly prodded me for the truth about my obvious sadness, all the while telling me: "You can tell me anything; you are my friend, and you can trust me."

I eventually relented, not because Petar was my friend and I could trust him (we had just met twenty-four hours ago), but because I needed someone to talk to, and he was the only one there. He was leaving next week, never to be seen or heard from by me again, taking my secret emotional baggage with him. Over the next hour I opened up my soul to this for all intents and purposes total stranger. I told him everything: about my grandmother, about her passing, how much I miss her, my depression during holidays, and why I still insist on working holidays.

While I talked and at some points cried, Petar listened and consoled me. He asked, "My friend, why didn't you spend the holidays with your family?"

I explained that I love my family and did not want to break down in front of them and be a burden.

He quickly responded, "My friend, they are your family, and I'm sure they may be going through similar emotions during this time of year. My friend, you and your family understand each other and could comfort one another; I doubt you would ever be considered a burden to your loved ones."

What Petar said made perfect sense and gave me a lot to think about. We talked back and forth for a while after that. Talking to him about my problems turned out to be very therapeutic. After I had finished, it was like a huge weight had been lifted from my shoulders. With eyes full of tears, I thanked him for listening, gave him a hug, and shook his hand. He graciously accepted my thanks and told me he was glad to be of assistance. He asked (tongue in cheek) for his compensation for our therapy session. He wanted a shot of tequila, and one for me too. I could not help but smile; I got him a shot (on me), but declined one for myself. I explained to him that I would love to do a shot with him, but knowing me, one shot would just be the beginning of tens of shots for me.

Petar said, "That sounds just fine to me; there's nobody here who cares!" I thanked him for his offer, but respectfully declined. Instead, I did a ceremonial toast with him using a shot of H2O.

Changing the subject, Petar told me about a unique situation that he wanted to get my personal perspective on.

"My friend, there was a Russian oligarch who would fly this one particular young lady from New Jersey to Moscow at least once a month. I would pick her up at LaGuardia Airport, she would be my only passenger, and I would fly her straight to Sheremetyevo International Airport. My friend, she would stay with the oligarch for forty-eight hours, and then I would fly her back. She would be given a hundred thousand dollars cash each trip. In addition, while there, the oligarch would take her shopping and buy her anything she wanted. My question to you, my friend, is why? Yes, the young lady was attractive, but there are plenty of attractive girls in Moscow, in Russia, in Eastern Europe, and elsewhere. My friend, what was so special about this particular girl? Why would this guy, who could virtually have his choice of any woman, do this?"

I started off stating the obvious: "Of course, I have never met the lady or the oligarch, so I'm going to draw on a personal experience to give my opinion. I have to use as a reference a person in my life, whom I have labeled my *Future Ex-Wife*.

"My Future Ex-Wife (FEW) was a platonic acquaintance, someone I knew years ago. I call her my FEW because I was in love with her and wanted to marry her despite knowing that the relationship was doomed to fail. The reason the relationship would definitely fail was, sad to say, I wasn't her type, and she never had and never will have any romantic feelings for me. Knowing that, till this very day, I know if she were to walk into my life and agree to marry me, I would probably do it. In my opinion, Olivia Wilde, Zoe Saldana, and Sofia Vergara (in no particular order) are the hottest women on the planet, but if I were in the company of my FEW, and one those three ladies, or all of them were to enter the room, I wouldn't even notice them.

"My FEW is captivating: an exotic beauty, extremely intelligent, with a great personality, and a courageous adventurer. Over the course of her young life she had been all over the world. It would be easier to list the places she hasn't gone than the places she has been to. When she travels to a locale, she doesn't go for just a couple of days, either. When I first met her, she was about to embark on a trip to Europe.

She stayed there for six months. She spent a month in Thailand and a couple of weeks in Costa Rica.

"I consider her courageous is because most of the time she travels alone. On numerous occasions, she tried, to no avail, to talk me into going with her on one of her trips. Each time I told her I couldn't afford it. Eventually she stopped asking. The last time I declined, she responded, "'f you wait until you can afford it, you'll probably never go anywhere.' In 2009, when I was watching the Disney movie *Up*, I couldn't help but think about her and relate to the characters Carl and Ellie Fredricksen in the movie.

"The most impressive thing about my FEW is that I have heard about egalitarians in theory, but my FEW is the only one I have ever come in contact with. During the time I knew her, she never referred to, described, or classified people using color or racial terms. She never made a derogatory statement that included a racial, ethnic, or religious slur, an endearing quality that we as a human race should all strive to emulate."

Petar chimed in, "My friend, she sounds wonderful. Why don't you try and find her and see if you can win her heart?"

I continued, "I haven't seen or heard from my FEW in over six years. A couple of years ago I found her on Facebook and sent her a friend request that she did not respond to. (And no, I am not a *creeper*.) I know that when you asked me the question about the oligarch and his 'Jersey girl,' you weren't eliciting a drawn-out account of my love life, but in my own way I hope to illustrate that sometimes people meet a love interest that stands head and shoulders above every other person we have ever known and ever will know."

Petar replied: "My friend, I get your point, but if that's the case, and the New Jersey girl is the *one* for the Russian oligarch; why doesn't he just marry her, or at least move her in with him?"

"Petar, I don't know why they aren't together full time. Whatever it is, it's gotta be a *good* reason. What I do know from personal experience, is when you have waited your whole life to meet that special *one*, and circumstances exist that keep you from that person, you will do anything to not let them get away, even if that means having to settle for a part-time position in their life, because a little bit of that person is better than none."

I spent the majority of my shifts on Thursday and Friday hanging out and talking to Petar. He is a fun, smart, and extremely generous person. I appreciated all the tips he gave me, and I actually felt guilty for accepting the money from him. Hanging out with Petar was one of the rare occasions when I felt it should be the other way around: I should have been the one tipping him.

Saturday (Christmas Day) I was off, and the hotel bar was closed, so I invited Petar to come and hang out and have a drink with me at a local bar that was open on Christmas Day. He accepted my invitation. We hung out Saturday night and had a blast. Petar is a "wild and crazy guy!"

I did not see him at all on Sunday. Monday morning he stopped by the bar for a few minutes before he headed off to his appointment with the aviation company. He thanked me for taking him out on Saturday and told me he had an awesome time. He followed up by saying that he no longer considered me "his friend," that I was much more—I was his "brother from another mother!" We both laughed and gave each other a big hug. We friended each other on Facebook, and I told him to make sure he stayed in touch. If Petar lived in St. Louis or I lived in Zurich, I am positive we would be the best of friends. No matter where Petar is in this world, he will always be "my friend."

TWELVE-DOLLAR BURGER

How you know where I'm at when you haven't been where I've been, understand where I'm coming from?

-Cypress Hill

I am a six-foot four-inch black male, I weigh about 250 pounds, and I have an average athletic build. I hate shaving because I suffer from *pseudofolliculitis barbae,* aka *shaving bumps,* so I shave at the most twice a month. Most of the time when I go shopping, to the gym, to get some food or for almost anywhere, I dress comfortably, and for me comfortably is old gym shoes, sweats, and a t-shirt. During the cold months, I add a hooded sweater and a black skullcap to my wardrobe. I am well aware that when I cross paths with people who don't know me, whether while walking down the street, strolling through the mall, or navigating dark underground parking garages, I am a menacing, hulking figure. It bothers me when I pass women walking down the street and they clinch their purses tightly; when I walk up to an intersection and the first thing I hear is the locking of car doors; and when I look for my car in a parking garage and people who I come across seemed apprehensive and sometimes afraid of me.

One night, I was sharing my frustration with my girlfriend at the time. She looked at me with a devilish grin and sarcastically said, "Well, you know you're a *monster!*" Sensing that I wasn't appreciating her humor, she kissed me on the cheek, gently took my face into her hands, looked me in the eyes, and told me, "Babe, you're a big teddy bear, and if people got only a glimpse of the man I know you to be, they would see what I see in you."

In 2009, I became a first-time homeowner. (Thank you, first-time homeowner's tax credit!) One day, at my new building, I got into the elevator with my new neighbor and his little boy. Standing in the elevator and looking straight forward, I noticed in my peripheral vision that the little boy was looking up and staring at me with a curious expression on his face. I acknowledged his stare with a casual glance; he smiled and said, "Hi!"

I smiled back and said, "Hello, young man."

The elevator door opened, and he walked out of the elevator, looked back and said, "Goodbye."

From that day on, whenever the neighbor's little boy and I saw each other, we would exchange a heartfelt, jovial greeting. Over time, I started to notice that after crossing paths with him, I would be in a great mood, and the rest of the day, to any—and everyone I encountered, I would extend a heartfelt, jovial greeting also. I came to realize through the simple kind gesture of that child and our ensuing relationship, that my curmudgeonly disposition had played a big part in creating the apprehensive, scary undertones that existed when I walked up to an intersection, passed women on the street, and encountered people in not-too-well-lit underground garages; and that the possible key to relieving the scary undertones was for me to start initiating positive interactions by smiling and saying hello to people. So from then on, I made a concerted effort to smile and say hello to most of the people I encountered during the course of my day. Some people would reciprocate, some wouldn't, but it didn't matter, because it's not about them, it's about me being congenial to my fellow man.

"Prepare to be *busy*" is my mindset during the slow parts of my bar shifts. I do my best to make sure that all necessary prep is done and the bar is fully stocked, so if I get really busy I will have everything I need to serve and take care of my guests. Because of limited space at the bar, I can store only a limited amount of supplies, with the bulk of the bar supplies being stored in different areas in the hotel. Therefore, when I don't have any guest at the bars, I take that opportunity to scurry about the hotel and scrounge up supplies.

On one occasion, upon returning from a supply run, a guest who had just spent the last few minutes waiting for service at the bar confronted me in the lobby. He asked, "Are you the bartender on duty?" I told him I *was* the bartender on duty. I apologized for my absence from the bar and invited him to return to the bar where I could assist him.

He followed me back to the bar where I offered him a food menu and asked if he would like a drink. He declined the menu and ordered a double shot of scotch on the rocks. I made the drink right away, and as soon as I sat the drink down in front of him, he picked it up and drank the whole thing and asked for another double in the same glass with no extra ice. I obliged and poured him another double and proceeded to start him a tab.

This time around he took his time and sipped this drink and he asked me where I was earlier. Once again, I apologized for my absence, and I explained to him that I had slipped away to gather bar supplies.

I formally introduced myself and asked his name and where he was visiting from. He told me his name was Kevin. He and his wife were on vacation, and they were from Charlotte. Kevin was a tall, well-dressed, black gentleman, about six feet three inches, with a slender build. He said he played basketball in college and now he worked as an executive for a Fortune 500 company in Charlotte. I told him I had never been to Charlotte, but I had heard it was a nice place to live and raise a family. Kevin said, "I agree with everything you've heard about Charlotte. My wife and I love living there."

I asked, "Are you and your wife happy with our hotel, and are you enjoying your visit to St. Louis?"

Kevin finished his drink and asked for another double. He told me that he and his wife were very happy with their accommodations at our hotel, and that up until that day they were having a wonderful vacation.

He explained that he and his wife had a disagreement earlier, which escalated into an ugly fight. Both parties said nasty things they didn't mean. (At least, he *hoped* she didn't mean what she said.) He had left their room to get some air and give them both a chance to calm down.

I told him that I was so sorry to hear that, and I hoped that they could work things out soon and salvage what was left of their vacation. He thanked me for listening, told me I was a "good brother," and hoped I was right.

I asked him, "When was the last time you ate?"

He said, "I haven't eaten since yesterday."

I presented him one of our food menus and encouraged him to eat something, impressing upon him the need to have some food for fear he would get sick if he continued to drink without some sustenance in his stomach. (He had already drunk at least three double scotches on the rocks.) Kevin accepted the menu and ordered another scotch on the rocks, but this time just a single shot.

While Kevin was looking over the menu, ten large black men entered the lobby and made their way toward the bar. These guys were huge. The biggest member of the group looked to be at least six feet four inches, 270 pounds, and the smallest a bare minimum of six feet tall, 220 pounds. As they got closer to the bar, I observed they were all either wearing or carrying matching motorcycle jackets. Once they got to the bar, one of the guys in the group asked if we serve food at the bar. I told him yes and invited him and his companions to have a seat; I would get some menus for them to take a look at.

As I passed out menus to the group, I noticed that the majority of them had multiple visible tattoos on their arms, hands, and necks. I started them all off with glasses of water, took additional drink orders, made those drinks, and served them. Once I had them all set up, I invited them to take their time checking out our menu. I said, "If you have any questions, or if you need anything, please don't hesitate to ask, and when you're ready to order, let me know."

I returned to check on Kevin and see if he was ready to place his food order. Kevin, speaking very quietly, commented on how they looked like a scary bunch, and that he wouldn't want to cross them and piss them off. He asked if they were hotel guests, and if there was some kind of bikers' convention in town. I replied that I wasn't aware of any bikers' convention in town. I didn't know if they were hotel guests, but that as far as I could tell, they seemed to be okay. I took Kevin's food order: a burger, medium-well, with Swiss and American cheese, bacon, and French fries.

After placing his order, I returned to the new group to see if everything was okay and if they were ready to place their food order. One of the guys commented on how expensive our food items on the menu were. He wanted to know, "What's up with you charging *ten dollars for just a burger?*" He went on to tell me they were from Ohio, and none of them had ever paid ten dollars for a hamburger.

I told them that I was just an employee of the hotel, and that I had no input or power when it comes to the pricing scale at the hotel. Also, after I added in taxes, the total price for the burger was actually around twelve dollars.

They all replied in unison, "*Twelve dollars for a hamburger? That sh*t's crazy!*"

Another member of the group chimed in, "I get it, I understand that you don't personally set the prices, but *damn,* can you explain to us why someone would pay twelve dollars for a f*ckin' hamburger, excuse my French?"

I asked the guys to hear me out and please bear with me, and I'd do my best to explain.

A lot of fast food restaurants sell a quarter pound burger. Let's use that fast food burger as a comparison to our burger. With a fast food quarter-pound burger, the burger patty weighs a quarter of a pound precooked. Our burger patty weighs one half of a pound precooked; it's twice as big. Most fast food restaurants precook their burger patties in quantity and warm them up per order. Our burgers are cooked to order. Most fast food restaurants serve their burgers well-done. With our burgers the guest can choose if their burgers are medium-rare, medium, medium-well, or well-done. At most fast food restaurants, if you want cheese on your burger, it costs extra. We don't charge extra for cheese, and we have different varieties of cheese to choose from: American, Swiss, cheddar, and Monterey Jack. If you want French fries with your burger at a fast food restaurant, it costs extra. Our burger comes with a free side order: French fries, potato chips, coleslaw, a fruit cup, or a side salad.

Right as I was almost done justifying the cost of our burger, Kevin yelled across the bar, "What's up with my food order?" All the guys at the bar turned their attention to him. Kevin had been listening in on the conversation between the guys and me. He yelled, "You wouldn't think if a person paid twelve dollars for a burger, it should take this long to get it."

I stepped back and addressed both the guys and Kevin. I explained, "Kevin ordered his burger medium-well; to create a good-tasting medium-well burger, you need to cook that raw beef patty for twelve to fifteen minutes to get a brown color outside and a temperature of 140 to 145 degrees at the center of the patty. We do our best to give you the quality burger of your choice. Now if you guys will excuse me, it's been about ten minutes; I'm going to go check on the status of the gentleman's order."

I went up to the kitchen, and there it was: Kevin's burger. The cook had just put it in the window, and it looked delicious. So when I got back to the bar, I made a point to carry Kevin's burger in my left hand. That way it would be on display between me and the guys who were on my left as I passed. I served Kevin his burger. He looked at the burger; then he looked at me, smiled, and said, "*Wow*, that looks good!"

As Kevin dug in, I went back to the guys and asked if they were ready to place an order. One of the guys asked what Kevin got. Kevin yelled across the bar to the guys, "This one of them twelve-dollar burgers and this *sh*t* is *good!*" It was a literal example of conspicuous consumption. All ten guys in the group ordered burgers; they all wanted their burgers exactly like Kevin's.

I placed their order, and while we waited for the food to be prepared, some of the guys stepped away from the bar to run up to their rooms, go to the restroom, or to step outside and have a cigarette. That dwindled the ten down to two: Mike and Chris. I took that opportunity to get to know the guys at the bar a little bit. I asked jokingly if they were the black version of SAMCRO. Both Mike and Chris told me they didn't know who or what SAMCRO is. I told them that SAMCRO stands for "Sons of Anarchy Motorcycle Club, Redwood Original." That's what a fictional motorcycle gang in the TV show *Sons of Anarchy* call themselves.

When I said "Sons of Anarchy," they immediately knew what I was talking about. They told me they had both seen the show and liked it, but they were not a motorcycle *gang*, they were a motorcycle *club*.

I quickly apologized and told the guys that I meant no disrespect. Mike told me everything was cool and that a lot of people's first impression of them is that they are a motorcycle gang. He went on to explain that the only things they have in common with the fictional motorcycle gang in Sons of Anarchy are their love of motorcycles and their love to ride.

Mike told me that their club started off with him, Chris, and a couple of other guys. They had all been childhood friends. Over time, a few friends of friends joined the club and became members. In the club's early years, they would meet and hang out at each other's homes, but about five years ago, the founding club members got together, got a loan, and bought an old gas station-garage, rehabbed it themselves, and turned it into their clubhouse. Their clubhouse is where the members hang out, drink beer, and socialize. They also use it as a place to work on and customize their bikes and assist each other making repairs they may need help with.

Their members are a diverse group who come from different walks of life. Some are current and ex-military. They have members who are small business owners, they have doctors, lawyers, and even a tattoo artist. They each pay monthly dues, which they use to pay the clubhouse's utilities, taxes, and upkeep, and they also buy tools they all use and share.

As I continued to listen and learn about the motorcycle club, I could not help but feel a little ashamed and embarrassed for prejudging the guys. They are nothing like what I thought they would be like; they are actually interesting and pretty cool.

The rest of the group started to return to the bar, so I broke away to get their burgers. While they were eating, Kevin made his way over to the group, introduced himself, and asked the guys if they were enjoying those twelve-dollar burgers. Then he ordered another double scotch on the rocks and asked the guys if they liked scotch. Mike said he had never tried scotch. Kevin instructed me to give all ten of the guys scotch on the rocks and put it on his tab. All the guys thanked Kevin and told him that he didn't have to do that. He insisted, though, and told them he would not take no for an answer.

As the guys enjoyed their lunch and sampled the scotch, Kevin mingled and talked with the group, sharing with them that he was from the "dirty South," that he was vacationing with his wife, and they were having a good time until "she started acting like a *bitch*," whereupon he decided to strike out on his own and have some fun.

A couple of the guys said they could sympathize with Kevin, which is why they left their wives at home. Everybody at the bar started laughing! In a show of unity, some the guys reciprocated and bought Kevin a couple of drinks. Then Kevin insisted on buying the whole group another round of drinks.

Everybody was having a good time. The only negative was that once Kevin downed a few more drinks, he started talking some crazy, offensive kind of Ebonics that included the *n-word*, used as the noun, the verb, the adjective, and the adverb in every sentence. A few of the guys, myself included, were turned off by Kevin's excessive use of the n-word, but we all cut him slack because we knew he was still upset about the argument he and his wife had and he was a little drunk. We just chalked it up as a party foul.

As the day turned into the evening, some of the group and Kevin decided to go out and check out some of the city's local bars. I suggested an area of town known as the Landing. It's within walking distance from the hotel (nobody would have to drive), and there are multiple bars and nightclubs to choose from. Kevin paid his tab, which was a little over three hundred dollars, and he tipped me 33 percent. I don't know if he was generous, drunk, or just trying to show off in front of the guys from Ohio. All I knew was that times had been tough and his generous tip was welcomed and much needed.

I got the guys from Ohio their bills, they all paid individually, and they pretty much tipped me 20 to 25 percent across the board. I definitely appreciated it. So about half the guys from Ohio, with Kevin in tow, headed to the Landing. As they left, I quoted a line from the TV show *Hill Street Blues*: "Hey—be careful out there!"

The next afternoon, three of the guys from the Ohio group came to the bar for lunch. The first thing they said when they sat down was, "You got some of those twelve-dollar burgers for us today?"

My answer was, "For you guys, most definitely!"

As the guys ate their lunch, I inquired about their previous night out with Kevin. They started to laugh and told me: "Your boy Kevin was a trip."

"My *boy*?" I answered. "He didn't go out with me; he went out with you guys, thus he is *your* boy."

One of the guys said, "Your boy, my boy, it doesn't matter. That dude is a *trip!*"

He went on to tell me that as soon as they left the hotel and started walking to the Landing, Kevin started being a jerk. Every woman they passed who had a pulse he hit on, and once they got to the first and only bar they went to on the Landing; he started acting stupid, and wanted to fight everybody at the bar. After a couple of hours, they had enough and wanted to go. They started to leave without Kevin, but they felt responsible for him because he had bought them drinks all night, and he did come with them, so they grabbed up Kevin and came back to the hotel. Once they got back to the hotel, a couple of their friends took Kevin to his room; they reported, "He pissed in the elevator on the way to his floor."

I told the guys, "That's horrible and disgusting."

They told me they totally agreed with me.

Fifteen minutes later, Kevin showed up with a young lady who I assumed was his wife. He made a point to sit at the far end of the bar, away from the Ohio guys. When I approach the couple, I could tell that Kevin seemed a bit nervous. He quickly introduced himself as if this was the first time we met. I caught on quickly that he didn't want his wife to know that we had met, and he had been at the bar most of the day yesterday.

I said, "Hello, sir, welcome to the hotel bar. Would you and your lady friend like to see a lunch menu today?" My actions let Kevin know that I understood the gravity of the situation, and that I wasn't going to tell his secret. When he realized that, a huge sigh of relief consumed his face.

His wife told me that they just wanted drinks, and she asked if they could take their drinks up to their room. I told her, "That's definitely okay."

I made their drinks, Kevin paid the bill, and left me a 100 percent tip, which his wife noticed and questioned him about aloud. He explained to her that I seemed like a "good brother," and he just wanted to hook me up.

As they walked away, she commented to him, "All he did was made us one drink; how does that make him such a good brother that deserved that much for a tip?"

After Kevin and his wife left, I returned to the section of the bar where the guys from Ohio were sitting and told them what just happened with Kevin and his wife. One of the guys said he thought it was messed up that Kevin didn't acknowledge them and say hello, and that he thought Kevin was a "*fake ass dude!*"

I told the guys that in my humble opinion, the Kevin we met the day before was a guy who had a fight with the woman he loved, he was upset about it, and he had way too much to drink. Today was a new day, he and his wife made up, and he was sober. He probably feels guilty about the way he behaved, and he most definitely does not want his wife to find out. If she knew just a portion of what he did, that knowledge could ruin their fragile reconciliation.

Another one the guys chimed in and said, "Kevin could have come over and said hello, and we wouldn't have snitched on him to his ole lady."

I told them that I didn't think that they would have snitched on him, and I think Kevin shares my opinion, but he doesn't know for sure. I told them, "with everything that's at stake, he would rather dis you guys than risk it. 'Causes guess what? After today, he'll probably never see you guys again, but his wife: he's gotta live with her. I'm sure Kevin is doing everything in his power to make sure 'what happens in St. Louis *stays* in St. Louis!'"

I could tell that the guys were coming around to my way of thinking, even if they didn't go so far as to admit it. I told the guys that I was happy that I had a chance to meet them, and that I learned a lot from them. One of the guys thanked me for my praise, but admitted he didn't know quite what I had learned from them. I came clean, and told him that when I first saw them, I thought they were a bunch of hoodlums who were gonna start trouble at the bar—a prejudgment that I'm ashamed to admit, but one that I am happy I was wrong about.

One of the guys told me, "Don't worry about it. We get that a lot, and it really doesn't bother us, because to those people who don't know me, but prejudge me, I say to them, as the rapper Rocko says in the chorus of one of his songs, "You just do you, *uma do me.*" As the guys left the bar, I told them thanks for stopping by and take care. They told me to do the same.

Now, whenever the guys from Ohio are in town, whether just one of them or any number of the group, they stop by, even if they aren't staying at my hotel, to say, "What's up?" and to have one of our twelve-dollar burgers.

FROM SCRIBNER WITH LOVE

Me and you, and you and me, No matter how they toss the dice, it had to be. The only one for me is you, and you for me, So happy together.

—*The Turtles*

The Nebraska Territory was an organized, incorporated territory of the United States. Nebraska officially joined the union and became the thirty-seventh state on March 1, 1867. Its capital is Lincoln, and its biggest city is Omaha, hometown to St. Louis Cardinals Hall of Famer Robert (Bob) Gibson.

I personally have never been to Nebraska, but I do know that football is extremely popular in that state, especially *Cornhusker* football! *Cornhusker* is the name given to the several sports teams at the University of Nebraska—Lincoln. The name *Cornhusker* first appeared in the school newspaper as "We Have Met the Cornhuskers and They Are Ours" referring to a 20-18 upset victory over Iowa in 1893. During the 1899 football season, Nebraska State Journal writer Charles "Cy" Sherman started referring to the team as Cornhuskers, and the name became popular and stuck until the present. The Cornhusker football program is the winningest NCAA Division I team for the past fifty years. The Cornhuskers have won five national championships: three under Dr. Tom Osborne, and two under Bob Devaney.

On a shift on December 12, 2012, a gentleman came to the bar decked out in Nebraska Cornhuskers attire. He had on a Cornhuskers hat, jogging suit, t-shirt, socks, and shoes. The reason I remember that specific date is it was a week after the Big 12 championship game. Ndamukong Suh had a monster game for Nebraska. (The St. Louis Rams were considering drafting him number one overall the following April, 2010.) Texas beat Nebraska 13-12, in a controversial Texas win.

I also remember that day because of the lasting impression our Cornhuskers visitor to the bar had on me. When he sat at the bar, I asked him (tongue-in-cheek): "Let me guess—you're a fan of the Nebraska Cornhuskers?"

He smiled and responded, "How did you ever figure that one out?"

I got him a beer and asked him, "What did you think about the Big 12 championship game last week?"

With a sly look on his face, he told me, "You don't want to open up that Pandora's Box and get me started."

His name was Cliff, and he was a devout Cornhuskers fan. If you cut him, he would bleed scarlet and cream. Cliff had been a Cornhusker fan for as long as he could remember, and so had his father before him. Cliff and I spent the next hour or so talking about the Big 12 championship game the Saturday prior. Of course, he was convinced beyond a doubt that Nebraska had been cheated out of the game.

He asked whether I was a Mizzou fan, being that I live in Missouri.

I told him, "Yes, I live in St. Louis and consider it my home, but I was born and raised in Illinois, so I'm an Illini fan." The conversation turned to professional football, and it turned out that both Cliff and I were St. Louis Rams fans. We started talking about all the recent Cornhuskers that have played for the Rams: Grant Winstrom, Toby Wright, and Tim Couch, just to name a few.

Cliff told me that he and his wife were headed home from Joliet, Illinois. They had gone there to visit their niece, and instead of driving straight through, they decided to stop in St. Louis for a couple of days. He comes from a small city called Scribner, in Dodge County, Nebraska. The town has a population of 947 people. Cliff has lived in Scribner virtually his whole life. He has been married for twenty-five years to the girl of his dreams. He fell in love with her the first time he saw her, and they have been together since they were both in junior high school. He owns the local grocery store in Scribner, which he bought from his father, who now works for him in the store. The store has been in his family for fifty years. Cliff explained that the only reason his little family-owned store has survived and stood the test of time is because there isn't another store in town, and the closest grocery store is twenty minutes away. Also, his store home-delivers food orders and heating oil to his customers.

I really liked Cliff and learning about life in Scribner. He hung out and we talked for a couple of hours. When my shift ended, I invited him back the next day to watch the Rams game. He thanked me for my hospitality and told me, "I just might take you up on your offer."

The next day, Cliff *did* take me up on my invitation to watch the Rams game. He came down to the bar accompanied by his wife, Claire a sweet lady. The two of them together were a joy to observe. They reminded me of Archie and Edith Bunker from *All in the Family*, minus the negative racial undertones and chauvinistic sarcasm. If you spent any time around them, you could tell how much the two of them loved and respected each other.

Claire told me the two of them had known each other for forty years and had been married for the last twenty-five years. Cliff was the first boy she ever kissed. The kiss occurred when they were in the eighth grade together. She was not as into Cornhusker's football as Cliff (who could be?), but she is Cliff's number one fan. She supports him faithfully, and he absolutely adores her. I really enjoyed the day spent with them, watching football and learning about their wonderful life together.

In April of 2012, I saw Cliff during Easter weekend for the first time since 2009. I was pleasantly surprised that he remembered me, and he was flabbergasted that I remembered him, his wife, and most of the things he shared with me that weekend over two years ago. I told him, "I always remember the really good people I meet," which is the honest to God truth.

He told me that his wife had passed away a year ago; I gave him my sincere condolences. He thanked me and told me he misses her, but every day things get a little better. I didn't get an opportunity to talk to Cliff during his short visit to St. Louis. I was off work the rest of the week.

Cliff and Claire were good people. They introduced me to a piece of Americana that I did not know still existed in this new millennium, and I must say, it was a pleasant treat to find out about it.

ANONYMITY

We're not against rap, we are not against rappers, but we are against those thugs.

—*Calvin Butts*

Till this day, I can still remember the first famous person I ever met. His name was Ernie "the Big Cat" Ladd. Ernie Ladd was a pro football player and a pro wrestler whom my mother dated for a brief time when I was eight years old. At the time, I had no idea Mr. Ladd had once played pro football for the San Diego Chargers, Houston Oilers, and the Kansas City Chiefs, respectively. I knew he was a wrestler, but that wasn't a big deal to me because I wasn't a fan of his, truth be told. I had never heard of him before my mother introduced me to him. It never seemed to bother Mr. Ladd that I was pretty much oblivious to who he was; in fact it was amusing to him. My favorite wrestlers were Jimmy "Superfly" Snuka, Dick the Bruiser, and the Junkyard Dog. The first time I met him, I remember thinking to myself, this guy is huge; he must be a giant. (He was six feet nine inches and over three hundred pounds.) Whenever he was around, I was always on my best behavior. I didn't want to do anything to upset him. It turned out I was right: Mr. Ladd was a giant, a *gentle* giant, who was very kind to my mother and me.

RIP, Ernie Ladd (November 28, 1938–March 10, 2007).

A *sports fan* is defined as an enthusiastic devotee of sports. I am a huge sports fan. I know everything about my favorite teams and favorite players, past and present. I want to make it clear: I am not like the character Gil Renard, played by Robert DeNiro in the movie *The Fan*. I consider myself to be more like Tony Reali, the host of *Around the Horn*.

I used to work at an adult club that quite a few professional athletes frequented. (More about this in the upcoming book *Impromptu*.) I was the biggest fan of one Hall of Fame football player who was there pretty often. I started following this athlete's career when he was in college, mainly because I thought his college team's uniforms were cool, and he was the best player on their team. He went on to be a great pro and to be elected to pro football's Hall of Fame. One night, when he was in the club, to my chagrin, one of my co-workers told him that I was a huge fan of his, and I would "just die" if I could meet him.

He looked at me, then told her, "Why the f*ck would I want to meet him?" To say that my feelings were hurt is an understatement, but those feelings were quickly replaced with disgust for him. Over the next couple of years, whenever I had the displeasure of serving this not-so-very-nice individual, ninety percent of the time he was rude to me and to my co-workers. As a matter of fact, the only people I ever observed him being kind to were our managers, who pretty much gave him carte blanche to anything he wanted that was in their power to give, and every attractive girl (he preferred blondes) he wanted to score with. He was not the first and he won't be the last celebrity that I will meet that is not a very nice person, aka an "A hole". That's why I personally prefer to keep my distance from celebrity patrons at establishments where I am employed. I would rather maintain a positive opinion of them and not find out they are jerks.

At my most recent job, my day at work starts at 10:30 a.m. The hotel bar officially opens at 11:00 a.m., so every day that gives me about thirty minutes to set the bar up, a job that consists of filling the two soda ice bins with ice, wiping down all the bar surfaces, unlocking the beer coolers and the liquor cabinets, then putting out the alcohol and red wine bottles for display and distribution. While setting up the bar, if a guest has a question, wants to buy something to drink or eat, or needs any assistance, I do my best to accommodate him.

On one Friday day shift, as I entered the lobby and headed to the bar, I noticed the lobby was empty except for one gentleman who was pacing back and forth and having an animated conversation on his cell phone. From a distance, he appeared to be of Latino descent: his hair was black and in pigtails that came down to his shoulders, and he was wearing a white jogging suit, with white high-top sneakers.

As soon as I stepped behind the bar, he recognized that I worked there, and with a sense of urgency, he approached the bar. Once he got up close, I noticed that the jacket of his jogging suit was unzipped, exposing a white t-shirt that read "Vote or Die." He had several gold chains of different lengths and thickness. Hanging on a couple of the chains were symbols and medallions that by my best estimation were gold, with some of the biggest diamond studs that I had ever seen. The sleeves to his jacket were pushed up just below his elbows, exposing his heavily tattooed forearms.

He stopped talking on his cell phone for a few seconds and asked if he could have a small soda, then went back to talking on the phone. I told him no problem and that the sodas were $2.50, as I reached for a sixteen-ounce pilsner to put the soda in. He stopped talking on the phone and told me he didn't want very much soda; one of the small plastic cups that he could see behind the bar would do fine. I told him that the sodas are the same price no matter what receptacle I use, and he would get more value for his money if I put his soda in a sixteen-ounce glass rather than in an eight-ounce plastic cup. He told me, "No disrespect, but the small cup is fine."

So I put the soda in the eight-ounce plastic cup and presented it to him. He went to reach in his pocket to get money to pay me, but before he could, I told him, "No charge, it's on the house."

He stopped talking on the phone to tell me that he appreciated it, but it wasn't necessary, he could pay for it.

I told him that I didn't feel comfortable charging him $2.50, considering how little soda he actually wanted. I insisted there would be no charge.

He thanked me, then reached in his pocket and pulled out a handful of hundreds, fifties, twenties, plus a few other denominations of bills, enough to choke a goat, and tipped me five one-dollar bills. I quickly assured him that the tip was not necessary and that I wouldn't feel right accepting it.

He looked me straight in the eyes and told me I had to accept the tip; he *insisted*. He drank the soda in one gulp and went back to talking on the phone. I thanked him, and he acknowledged me with a hand gesture and went back to pacing all around the lobby.

I went back to setting up and prepping the bar, but I must admit my curiosity was tweaked. I couldn't help but wonder who he was. Who would carry that much cash? All I knew is that he was very nice and generous; and I hoped his patronage was a sign that I was going to have a good day.

On this particular day it took me a little longer than usual to get the bar set up, but after forty-five minutes I was finished. Right on cue, the cell phone guy came back to the bar, but this time he ordered a cocktail. I got him his drink. He paid me with a twenty-dollar bill and told me to keep the change. He did this about three times over the course of an hour: got a drink, paid me with a twenty-dollar bill, told me to keep the change, and went back to talking on the phone and pacing about the lobby.

The next time he came up to get his drink, he wasn't on the phone. After I served him, he commented on what a beautiful day it was, and asked if he could take his drink with him out onto the hotel patio that is adjacent to the bar. I told him that it was okay to do so. After fifteen minutes or so had passed, I took some initiative, made him another drink, and delivered it to him outside on the patio. He thanked me for "lookin' out," took the drink, paid me with a twenty-dollar bill, and par for the course, told me to keep the change.

I told him how much I appreciated his generosity, and that I would be back in fifteen or twenty minutes to check on him and see if he needed anything. He said that wouldn't be necessary. "It's hot as hell out here. I'm coming back in to chill at the bar." We both returned inside to the bar, he had a seat on one of the bar stools, and I assumed my usual position behind the bar. I offered him a food menu, which he respectfully declined.

The TV at the bar was on a sports channel, and the topic of discussion was Barry Bonds and the grand jury indictment against him. The cell phone guy asked me what I thought about this whole Barry Bonds steroid thing.

I replied that the only people who know for sure if Bonds cheated and did steroids are God, Bonds, and his childhood friend, Greg Anderson.

The cell phone guy said, "No matter what, I don't think Bonds should go to jail for cheating and using steroids, 'cause he most definitely wasn't the only one usin' that sh★t! To prosecute only him, basically making him the scapegoat for the entire steroid era in Major League Baseball, is not fair, and it just ain't right!"

I told him I agree, and that "Last time I checked, there isn't a shortage on real bad guys doing real bad things. I'm sure society would be better served if the Federal government used that time and those resources to pursue those people."

Starting to feel a little comfortable with my guest, I asked him where was he from. He told me he was born and raised in Cleveland, Ohio. I told him that my great grandfather's name was Cleveland Rencher, and that growing up I always thought of Cleveland as a person, not a city. I asked him how he was enjoying his stay in St. Louis, and if his accommodations at our hotel were to his liking.

He said, "I'm in town for only a couple of days, so I haven't seen any of the city, but so far I've definitely enjoyed my stay at this hotel."

I asked if he was in town for business or pleasure. He responded that his business is his pleasure. He is in the music industry, and he did a show at Pop's the night before.

Pop's is a saloon and music venue across the Mississippi River, in Sauget, Illinois. It's about five minutes by taxi from downtown St. Louis. Pop's opened in 1981, and is known throughout the music industry. Rock groups such as Quiet Riot, Foghat, and Buckcherry, and solo artists like Bob Bell have at one time in their careers graced the stage at Pop's.

I told my guest I thought it was cool he played Pop's, and I asked, "How did your show go?"

He said, "We rocked the house. We had a good crowd, and it turned out to be fun for everyone."

I told him that sounded awesome! Then I admitted that I didn't recognize him or know his name, and the only recording artists I knew of from Cleveland, were Bone Thugs-n-Harmony.

He smiled and told me, "That's my peeps." He is Bizzy Bone, of Bone Thugs-n-Harmony. (I was excited!)

"Man, it's good to meet you! I *love* Bone Thugs-n-Harmony. You guys' music is the *sh*t*."

Bizzy thanked me for all the love-givin to Bone, Thugs, and their music; they really appreciate it.

Then I came clean and told Bizzy that even though I am a fan of Bone Thugs' music, I am ashamed to admit that I didn't know any of the group members' names other that they all have Bone as their surname, and until then, I didn't know what any of the members of the group look like—no disrespect.

Bizzy quickly replied, "No disrespect taken," and added, "After you've been in the celebrity game for a while, you appreciate the few opportunities for anonymity." He adamantly stated that he loved and appreciated his fans, but he missed the days of being able to go public places and just relax without being pursued by autograph seekers or worse yet wannabe TMZ type paparazzi.

"Cool, I understand," I told him. "I had no idea that Bone Thugs-n-Harmony were in town playing at Pop's."

He explained that actually they weren't. He was in town on his own, doing his own thing, performing his own stuff. He is heavily involved in underground hip-hop. Most of the stuff he is working on now you most likely won't hear on the radio, but you might hear it at nightclubs.

Bizzy hung out at the bar, having a few drinks, and we talked about sports, social issues, and music for most of the day. He was one the most down-to-earth people I had ever met. It was like hanging out and talking to an old friend you haven't seen in a while. He was up-to-date on current events, both foreign and domestic, and to my surprise, he had a huge and diverse love and knowledge of music. At one point, he played Beethoven's Sixth Symphony on the bar using only his hands and the actual bar as his flaccid instrument.

For most of the day Bizzy was my only customer. Around 3:00 p.m., another gentleman came to the bar and eventually joined us and our multiple-topic conversation. Let's just call him Fred he's a carpenter from Arkansas. He and his family came to town for a summer vacation. Bizzy introduced himself and told him he was a member of Bone Thugs-n-Harmony. Unfazed, Fred told him that he had never heard of him, his group, or heard *any* of their songs. He listens only to country.

Believe it or not, Bizzy liked the fact that Fred didn't know him and had never heard any of his music, and he respected Fred's blunt honesty. Bizzy insisted on buying Fred whatever he wanted to drink. After a little prodding, Fred graciously accepted and ordered a beer. The guys and I hung out and talked for about an hour. Bizzy appeared to be having a great time. He really enjoyed just hanging out, being one of the guys.

While we were hanging out, another program on the sports channel started debating the Barry Bonds steroid issue. Fred chimed in that Bonds is a cheater and deserves whatever he gets.

Bizzy asked, "What about the other guys who cheated and took steroids? Bonds wasn't the only one; why should he go to jail?"

Fred begrudgingly admitted that he could see Bizzy's point, but reiterated that he had no sympathy for Bonds, whom he considered to be an *sshole.

Bizzy responded to Fred that he wasn't necessarily for or against Bonds, but he was curious why Fred felt so much animosity toward Bonds. He asked Fred whether he ever had met Bonds, and Bonds had disrespected him in some way, or had Bonds done something to one of Fred's family members. Fred told us that he personally had never met Bonds, but one of his carpentry union members had done some work on one of Bonds's houses and the carpenter told Fred that Bonds was a jerk.

Fred also thought that Bonds was an egotistical maniac who wasn't a good teammate. Fred formed this impression because he had heard a rumor that while Bonds was with the San Francisco Giants, he had his own locker room, separate from the rest of the team.

Bizzy, wearing his diplomat's hat, reminded us that he, along with all the parties present, had never met Bonds, and that none of us were 100 percent sure about whether Bonds had a private locker room. He said that in his humble opinion, playing professional sports is entertainment, thus the athletes can be considered entertainers, and if all present accept that perception, he would like to share his knowledge as a professional entertainer himself.

He explained that when he is on the road doing shows, it is a standard part of his contracts with the promoters of his shows for him to have a private dressing room. Bizzy was quick to distinguish that it's not because he is a prima donna, but because before each show, he needs absolute silence for at least an hour, so he can calm his mind, gather his thoughts, and prepare mentally to give the best show possible. He has tried other disciplines, all in hopes of achieving the serenity necessary to put on a great show, but the most effective way has been the hour alone in absolute silence in a private dressing room. So with that in mind, what if Bonds is similar? Some people say that hitting a baseball at the Major League level is the hardest thing to do in professional sports. So maybe, just maybe to perform at a high level and be a successful hitter, he needs that time alone, in his own locker room, to get mentally prepared—just sayin'.

Fred finished his beer, shook Bizzy's hand, and thanked him for the beer. He shook my hand and thanked both of us for the good time and the interesting conversation. In parting, he told us that no matter what we say, he *still doesn't like Barry Bonds!* Bizzy and I told him goodbye, and we both extended well wishes to him and his family.

After Fred was gone, Bizzy told me he liked Fred, and even if we didn't change his mind, we still gave him another perspective to think about when it comes to Bonds. Bizzy finished his drink and said he was going to head up to his room to take a nap. Maybe later he would get out and about, and check out a little of St. Louis's nightlife. He double-checked to make sure he didn't owe anything. I told him his bar tab was all square and how much I appreciated his company and his generosity. He told me the pleasure was all his, adios, and take care. What an interesting shift, hanging out with a cool guy!

Despite my positive encounter with Bizzy, I am still apprehensive about meeting celebrities. Bizzy was great, but I have met far too many celebrities who remind me of the aforementioned Hall of Famer, whose name I will not reveal. I would, though, like to recognize a few celebs that were pretty cool: Jay Haas, Christopher "Big Black" Boykin, and a special *shout out* to DMX. It just happened that right before I met DMX, I had seen a not-so-flattering episode of *Behind the Music* about him. With that in mind, he was one of the nicest, most respectful, and generous people I have ever met. Every day during his brief stay at my hotel, he tipped the housekeeper who cleaned his room at least twenty bucks. He graciously signed autographs and took pictures with any and all staff members who asked. Whenever he was in the lobby, and one of the housekeepers were cleaning or straightening up, he would tell them that he appreciated the job they were doing and tip them twenty dollars. I delivered him room service and served him several times in the lobby. Each time, he was kind, generous, and patient, a real class act.

So to Bizzy, Big Black, DMX, and Jay, *thank you* so much for your patronage.

FUNNY MAN

Our lives begin to end the day we become silent about things that matter.

—*Martin Luther King*

When I was thirteen years old, I went to Rock Junior High School—a tough place, to say the least. What I remember the most about Rock was that in the seventh grade, for a brief time I had a nickname given to me by one of my peers: *Funny Man*. Back in those days we didn't have in our vocabulary or even know words like *fag, gay, homosexual,* or *queer* even existed, but the word we did have was *sissy*. To us, a sissy was a boy who behaved, walked, or talked like a girl. Something to take into account is that when I was thirteen years old, I—and for the most part most of the other boys—was asexual. We hated girls; we thought they were strange, and that they walked, talked, and behaved *funny*. So at that time, no thirteen-year-old boy wanted to be thought of as a sissy.

In the beginning of the seventh grade one of my classmates and I were making fun of each other, having harmless fun, but my teases were funny, and the crowd that had gathered were laughing at the other boy. So he got mad and took our teasing to an ugly level. He called me a sissy. Keep in mind no boy wanted the word sissy associated with him. The *laws of the schoolyard* at the time were such that if someone called you a sissy, you had to prove that you weren't one, which meant a knock-down-drag-out fistfight.

As soon as he said it, I should have immediately punched him in his face and kicked his ass, but I made a mistake: I didn't follow the laws of the schoolyard. So he took the teasing further. He said I was a sissy because I walked like a girl. Everyone present started laughing. So he continued and said I walked funny, so my name should be Funny Man. The other kids laughed and pointed at me and started chanting: "*Funny Man, Funny Man, Funny Man!*"

The nickname spread through the school like wildfire. I tried to contain it by enacting the laws of the schoolyard and fighting everyone who would call me that, but it was too late. The damage was done, and they wouldn't stop saying it.

Those were brutal times for me. I tried everything; I even mimicked the way Billy Dee Williams walked. Billy Dee Williams was a heartthrob during those days. Every little boy wanted to grow up to be him, and every little girl wanted to grow up to marry him. If I walked like Billy Dee, there would be no way anyone could say I was a sissy. It didn't matter. They wouldn't stop the teasing; they were relentless.

Eventually, due to time, the short attention span of kids, and the emergence of new foils, the teasing subsided. I didn't like being the focus of mob teasing, and from that point on in my life, I would never participate in that type of group behavior.

In September 2011, Jamey Rodemeyer, a gay teen who was being taunted, harassed, and bullied at school, committed suicide. Jamey Rodemeyer, you will never be forgotten; RIP.

I joined the United States Air Force when I was seventeen. My first duty station was at Lackland Air Force Base in San Antonio, Texas. On a Saturday at a local mall, I witnessed a group of men harassing a gay couple. They were following the young couple through the mall, taunting them with curse words and homophobic slurs. The scene was disturbing and unsettling to me; that ugly spectacle bothered me the rest of the day. Later that day, I ran into an older friend—let's just call him Sarge. He noticed that I wasn't my normal self and could tell something was bothering me. I told him about what had happened at the mall. He asked, "Why did it bother you?"

I told him that even though I didn't like gays, no one should be treated like that.

Sarge asked, "Why do you not like gays?"

I told him that I felt uncomfortable being around gays.

Really!

Why?

"I don't know. I just do."

Sarge asked, "Are you secure in your own sexuality?"

I asked him, "What do you mean? I like girls; I don't want to be with boys!"

He asked, "Are you sure?"

I angrily replied, "*Positive!*"

Sarge explained to me that persons who are secure in their own sexuality shouldn't be uncomfortable in the company of homosexuals. As he put it, "It doesn't rub off." He added that he feels that people who get angry at homosexuals are actually insecure in their own sexuality. It would be ironic if those guys at the mall who were attacking the gay couple were closet homosexuals, and that the hate they were directing toward the couple was the manifestation of the hate they felt for themselves.

After talking to Sarge, I went from being upset about what I had seen at the mall to questioning my own sexuality. He gave me a lot to think about. Was Sarge right when he said guys who don't like people who are gay are actually closet homosexuals? If that's true, was Sarge in a back door way trying to insinuate that I was gay? Is he right? *Am I gay?*

For the first time in my life, I asked myself some hard questions. Am I really attracted to women, or was I just claiming attraction to women because that's what society says I should feel? Am I physically attracted to men?

After honest and deep deliberation, I could not recall any time that I have ever had an urge to kiss a man, or felt any sexual arousal brought about by seeing any man. During basic training, I did not experience one erection. At the time, I thought the military had given us something to curb our sexual appetite, but as I think about it, I was around nothing but men during basic; that's why I never got aroused.

I admit that when I was younger I didn't like girls, but I did like women. At the time I didn't necessarily understand why, but I think it was the noticeable difference in their body compared to mine. As the girls in my age group got older and their bodies started to mature, I began to become attracted to them.

The verdict is in and it's unanimous: I like women! And using a famous line from Jerry Seinfeld: "Not that there's anything wrong with that." I'm not attracted to men. I was so happy and relieved: I'm *not gay!* I called Sarge and told him the good news. He listened to what I had to say, and told me he was happy for me and about my newfound sexual security. But he added, "Grasshopper, you still have a lot to learn about life and people."

What did he mean by "I still have a lot to learn about life and people?" And who the hell is Grasshopper?

Sarge was so right: I did have a lot to learn, and I know for a fact that without Sarge's sage advice at that time of my life, there is no guarantee that I would have ever been able to remove the albatross that of sexual insecurity from around my neck. Without that holding me back, I have been blessed to have had acquaintances and friends from the gay, lesbian, and bisexual community who are smart, loyal, exceptional people, and who have changed my life for the better just by my association with them. To this day, I feel deeply indebted to Sarge. His patience and wisdom definitely started me on a path of self-awareness and self-improvement. Thank you, sir.

> I've paid my dues time after time.
> I've done my sentence but committed no crime.
>
> —*Queen*

"Don't ask, don't tell" (DADT) was the official United States policy on homosexuals serving in the military from December 21, 1993, until September 20, 2011. The policy prohibited military personnel from discriminating against or harassing closeted homosexual or bisexual service members or applicants, while barring openly gay, lesbian, or bisexual persons from military service. Prior to its end, a lot of national and local news programs were discussing all aspects of homosexuality. At my local gym, one of the many highly debated water cooler topics was whether people are born gay, or if they choose to be gay. The discussions at times would become a little heated, with most opinions represented being the product of speculation. During that time period I met and befriended Ryan, an openly gay man, who stayed at the hotel I bartend at.

During Ryan's stay at the hotel, he and I had had many in-depth conversations about an array of social topics; no subject matter was off-limits. Because of this comfort level between us, I felt no apprehension telling Ryan about the gym debate and asking his opinion on whether homosexuality is a choice.

Without hesitation, Ryan started to tell me a little of his personal story. He was born and raised in Mississippi. He personally feels that the culture of the Deep South is predominantly anti-gay. So growing up, he had three strikes against him: He was gay, he was gay growing up in the South, and he was a gay white man growing up in the South who was attracted to black men.

He hid all this from his family, and when he was old enough, he joined the Navy. While in the Navy, he met someone and fell in love, but they were discovered and *outed*. Due to DADT, he and his partner were forced out of the Navy. The relationship ended, and his partner returned to his hometown.

Ryan had no money and nowhere to go, so he contacted his family and asked for help, but before they would help, they pressed for information about his abrupt and early exit from the Navy. Under unrelenting questions and pressure, he came clean and told them the truth about everything. His family was mortified and extremely angry. They told him they would do nothing to help him, that he was no longer a part of their family, that he was no longer welcome in their home, and to never contact them again. He wasn't surprised by their response, but it was still crushing.

He was homeless with no money, and admitted that for a short time he resorted to prostitution. He wasn't ashamed of the choice. He felt that he did what he needed to do to survive and that those tough times made him a stronger person.

That was twenty years ago. Since then he and his mother and father have reconciled, but till this day his brother still won't have anything to do with him. With a serious, staunch look on his face, he asked, "Do you think I would choose any of that?" He added he is more than happy with his life now. He has a good man in his life who loves him, good friends, and a great job. No, he does not believe homosexuality is a choice. As long as he can remember, he has always been attracted to men, and he was definitely born gay.

> I believe that a subconscious solidarity exists among people who have been prejudged or persecuted for something that is physically or mentally out of their control.
>
> —*C. D. Rencher*

A few years ago I saw an interview with Mahmoud Ahmadinejad, the president of Iran, where during the course of the interview he emphatically stated that there are no homosexuals in Iran. *B*llsh*t*. Excuse me while I climb on my soapbox.

I believe that people are born gay. If I'm right, homosexuals have been around as long as Homo sapiens have walked this earth. Studies exist showing that attraction to the same gender exists even in the animal kingdom. So if I'm right, being born gay is on the same level as being born a boy or a girl, being born with blonde hair or brown hair, being born with blue eyes or brown eyes. It all depends on what God's will is, not man's will. So to say there are no gay people in Iran is like me saying there are no gay professional football players. I don't know of any, but if my theory is right, there probably are.

> I don't care if gays get married; they should have the right to be miserable just like the rest of us.
>
> —*Peter Griffin*

In my short life, I have never seen homosexuality as socially acceptable in the United States as it is in this millennium. States like Iowa and New York have passed laws that allow same sex marriage, and other states recognize civil unions between same sex couples. This type of progress is good not only for the gay, lesbian, and bisexual community, but for the human race as a whole. It shows that tolerance and acceptance is taking root and growing in the human spirit. We still have a way to go, but I think we are on the right track.

Every year at my hotel, in the fourth quarter of the year, we host a group called the High Bear Nation. The High Bears are a gay social group consisting of like-minded mustached or bearded individuals who come together to share common interests and their love for one another. Most of their members are muscular to above average in size, which is why they are called Bears. The High Bears are some of the nicest people I have ever met. They are always courteous and generous to me. I attribute the positive interaction that exists between the High Bears and me to the fact that I am respectful, friendly, and nonjudgmental of them, and they reciprocate. A few of their members flirt with me, but I recognize it for what it is—harmless fun.

One day I had at least ten members during my shift ask for coffee "strong and black," just like they like their men. That was the ongoing joke of the day—no harm, no foul. When I observe High Bear Nation, the first word that comes to mind is *love*: love of one's self, love of one's partner and love of one's friends.

Sometimes during their visit, I reflect and think about Sarge and his patient mentoring of me. If only Sarge could see me now. I've learned a lot, I've still got a long way to go, but because of Sarge I'm headed in the right direction.

OUR FUTURE

And they said unto him, Hearest thou what these say? And Jesus said unto them, Yea; have ye never read, Out of the mouth of babes and sucklings thou hast perfected praise?

—*Matthew 21:16*

At the hotel I work at, the restaurant on the property is open seven days a week. It opens at 6:30 a.m. for breakfast; it shuts down at 2:00 p.m., right after lunch; and it reopens at 5:00 p.m. for dinner, and stays open until 11:00 p.m. During the restaurant's three-hour hiatus, the only place hotel guests can get food are from in-room dining (room service) or the lobby bar. From 11:00 a.m. till 11:00 p.m., the bartender serves food in the bar area and the lobby. When we get a patron at the bar who is accompanied by underage children, we invite them to be seated at one of our tables in the lobby. (It's a state law that no one under twenty-one years of age can sit at a bar that serves alcohol.)

When it comes to serving food, I prefer to serve pre-teen kids. They are almost always well-mannered (they say please, thank you, etc.), even if their parents aren't, and they are decisive when placing their orders (in comparison to most adults). When I think about the multitude of people I have taken care of and served food to, one remarkable young man stands out: Clay, an eight-year-old little boy who, along with his mom, I had the privilege of serving lunch to on one afternoon. What distinguished Clay from most children (actually, from most *people* I have waited on) was that he was so articulate and reserved, and these qualities were more amazing, because a child who was so young possessed them.

I approached their table, introduced myself, and inquired if they were interested in having lunch. Clay responded, "Hello sir, my name is Clay, and this is my mom. May we take a look at a couple of menus?" His mother just smiled, a subtle endorsement to what the little boy said.

As I retrieved a couple of menus and headed back to their table, I thought, *This kid is really mature, but he looks so young.*

I presented them the menus, and I asked the young man how old he was. He smiled and said, "Eight and a half."

I thought, *Eight and a half. Wow! That just makes his demeanor more impressive.*

They placed their order, and fifteen minutes later, when I was leaving the kitchen with their food in tow, I ran into Clay. He asked, "Is that our food?" I told him it was, he thanked me for getting their order so fast, told me he was headed to the restroom to wash his hands, but his mother was sitting at their table waiting for the food, and that he would join her shortly.

When I got to the table, I served the food. Before Clay returned, I told the mother how impressed I was with her son and that she should be commended for doing such a great job of raising him. She blushed bashfully and thanked me for my kind words. She told me that it's not easy, but she and her husband try to do their best. She said they are blessed to have him; he is a good kid.

Over that weekend, I ran into Clay and his mom a couple more times during their stay at the hotel. They told me that they are from Arkansas, and that they are rabid St. Louis Cardinals fans. Every year, they make it a point to come to St. Louis and see a game live. Young Clay was fluent beyond his years in Cardinals baseball lore.

A year later, an older gentleman approached me at the bar and told me his grandson recognized me and wanted to say hello. To my surprise, it was Clay. He remembered me from his last visit to my hotel. I was so flattered. Clay and his grandparents had lunch in the lobby that day. After they were finished, the grandparents sent Clay to pay me. Their bill was about twenty-five dollars; Clay paid me with a fifty-dollar bill and told me to keep the change. Clay's family has always been extremely generous, but I'm pretty sure his grandparents didn't intend for Clay to give me a twenty-five-dollar tip. I thanked him, but encouraged him to double-check with his grandparents before giving me that amount. Before the family left the area, they all came up to say goodbye. The grandfather gave me a handshake; in his hand was a ten-dollar bill. He whispered in my ear that Clay told him what I said about the change left over from the fifty, and he just wanted to thank me for being so honest. Clay's family was some of the nicest people I have ever met; all of them—the mom, the father, the grandfather, and the grandmother—were kind, generous, respectful people. No wonder Clay is the way he is. I can't see the future, but I wouldn't be surprised if Clay grows up to be successful at whatever he puts his mind to. Granted, life is not easy, but with the principles and morals his family is endowing him with, I have little doubt that he'll be able to jump over any hurdles, get around any hazards, and navigate any hardships he may encounter during this marathon of a journey we call life.

I subscribe to the analogy that children are like sponges. If you give them positive things like love, compassion, and education, just to name a few, they will absorb and retain most of it, and hopefully become assets to their community. If I'm right, that means that if you neglect them or do not shield them from negative influences, the consequences can be detrimental to them and to society as a whole.

Back in 2007 I saw a movie called *Alpha Dog*. The movie was based on a true story about a group of friends who are owed a drug debt by a rival who refuses to pay them. Desperate to claim the money, the friends come up with an ill-conceived plot to kidnap the fifteen-year-old brother of the rival and ransom him for the amount owed. They kidnap the young man and hangout and party with him, all the while introducing him to their friends and acquaintances as their kidnap victim. In time it dawns on the friends that there are serious consequences to kidnapping. They eventually make things worse when they decide to murder the young boy in hopes of covering up the kidnapping. In the beginning of the movie, the narrative states, "You can say that this is about drugs, or guns, or disaffected youth, or whatever you like, but this whole thing is about parenting, taking care of your children." As I watched this movie, those words kept playing over and over again in my head, and as the story unfolded, I recognized key things that happened because the perpetrators and their accomplices seemed oblivious to natural ideas of right and wrong. There were many opportunities for perpetrators, accomplices, or bystanders who were privy to what was going on, to step up and be the voice of reason, or to tell their parents or the authorities. If they had told some authority figure, maybe the heinous outcome could have been averted. But none of them were morally compelled or had the courage to do so.

After the young man was murdered, the people involved showed no remorse, just selfish fear about being implicated and possibly charged with the crime. The main characters in this movie (which is based on a true story) are all teenagers or in their early twenties. I ask myself, *were they just born bad?* But then I revisit the narrative at the beginning of the story and recall a saying, "There are no bad children, just bad parents."

In the beginning of 2008, I spent a lot of time alone, brooding. I was very unhappy about many aspects of my life, my past, my present, and my future prospects. I eventually came to the realization that I wasn't giving 100 percent effort to improve my life and reach my goals spiritually, health wise, intellectually, or professionally. I started praying every day, asking God to be my guide and to show me what I can do for him. I made a serious effort to eat healthier and work out more consistently. I started reading self-help books, and trying to implement what I learned into every aspect of my everyday life.

I got a second job in hopes of improving my finances, and with the objective of being able to afford a few things I dreamed of having. By 2009 I started to see a definitive, positive change in the direction my life was headed. I was encouraged by my relationship with God. I lost some weight and felt healthier than I had in a long time. Through reading, I had learned a lot of positive things I never knew, and I was able to fulfill a long-sought-after dream in buying a loft in downtown St. Louis.

During my first year at my new place, I met quite a few of the residents in my building, but to me they were all just acquaintances; I knew none of their names. I take ownership of that shortcoming: I was totally culpable for the fact that I did not have a more neighborly relationship with the people in my building. Right or wrong, I had my reasons for preferring my anonymity.

There was one person in my building who was not having it though, who refused to let me keep to myself. He was my next-door neighbor's two-year-old son. Every time he would see me or we would cross paths, he would say, "Hi! Hi! Hi!" and he would not stop until I returned the gesture. In the elevator, in the hallway, in the garage, it didn't matter. "Hi! Hi! Hi!" As he got older and his vocabulary grew, he asked my name and told me his. After he learned my name, every time he caught sight of me he would say, "Hi Celester." A lot of people have a hard time pronouncing my name correctly, but not this kid, sometimes I feel he enunciates my name better than I do. Through him, I met his parents, a very nice couple with a new baby on the way.

Over the past couple of years, I have been on the sideline observing my little friend grow up. After his mom brought a baby girl into the world, I ran into my young friend and his father in the elevator. He was carrying flowers his father had bought for his wife. As soon as they opened the door to their home, my young friend rushed through the door saying, "Mommy, Mommy! These are for you, Mommy!" Having these people as neighbors has definitely been a blessing. The family is a joy to be around.

In July 2011, I ran into my little friend's mom in the garage. We chatted for a few minutes. We both mentioned how we hadn't seen each other in a while, and I asked how the kids were. She told me they were fine, and matter of fact, just the other day she had asked her son if he had seen me recently. He said he hadn't, and he hoped that I am okay. Keep in mind he's only four. (He turned four in August.) The fact that such a young child would have the emotional capacity to express concern for me, a neighbor he barely knows, shows just how special he is.

On Christmas Eve of 2011, I was returning home from work feeling sad and alone, and I had a lot of things on my mind. I didn't mean to, but I walked by my neighbor's son, who was standing in their doorway, and I did not acknowledge him and say hello. As I went to open my door I heard his tiny voice say, "Hello, Celester." I turned and looked in his face. With no words, just an expression, he conveyed to me, "You are not alone; you have a friend in me." At that moment my spirits were uplifted. I smiled at him and I told him, "Hello, my friend, and merry Christmas to you and your family."

My mother and I talk on the phone a couple of times a week. A common theme of each of those conversations is current events and the local news. We talk for hours about the crime on our streets and how scary our world is becoming. We both either fear or at least are apprehensive about people and about going anywhere after dark. My mother thinks that it's horrible that hard-working, honest people are holed up, locked away in their homes. Afraid to go out, while the hoodlums have almost taken over, she feels it should be the other way around; they should be the ones locked away somewhere.

"Once in a blue moon", I'll be at home watching TV, and I can hear my neighbor's children coming and going, or just playing in the hallway. Sometimes when that happens, I mute the sound on the television and bask in the sound of their joyful voices. For those few glorious moments I am reminded that not everything outside my door is dark and gloomy.

I have no children of my own, and I have never personally been involved with the rearing of any child, so how can I judge any parent, when I have never walked in their shoes? Were Clay and my neighbor's son born the way they are, or are they products of kind, thoughtful people with good, strong moral values, and being raised in a happy, positive environment? All I know is that whenever I cross paths with my neighbor's new little girl, she says, "Hi! Hi! Hi!"

Post Script:

In June of 2009, Michael Jackson passed away. He was fifty years old. Over the span of four decades, Mr. Jackson amazed and entertained millions of people with his singing and dancing. He was recognized worldwide as the King of Pop. Over the course of his career, he sold hundreds of millions of albums. He was also a caring and generous person, who donated money and his time to various charitable endeavors. Despite all of Mr. Jackson's achievements, the latter part of his life was marred with innuendo and controversy. On more than one occasion Mr. Jackson had to defend himself in judicial court and in the court of public opinion against multiple allegations of sexually inappropriate behavior with children. Mr. Jackson was eventually exonerated of all charges, but right or wrong, the stigma of being a child molester dogged him for the rest of his life. Mr. Jackson has always adamantly denied all charges, admitting that yes, he did spend time with young children, but stating that his intentions were innocent and that he at times preferred the company of young children. Most adults considered the fact that Mr. Jackson liked hanging out with children peculiar to say the least. A lot of people speculated that since Mr. Jackson did not have a normal childhood, he was reliving his youth through his association with young children.

I have my own theory on why Mr. Jackson enjoyed the company of children. I personally do not spend hardly any time with or near young children, but on the few occasions when I am around children, I marvel at their level of energy, and their capacity for joy knows no bounds and is infectious. I find their innocent, brutal honesty refreshing, and I consider the unconditional love and friendship they extend to me to be priceless. They don't care about the color of my skin; they don't care if I'm wearing the latest brand name clothes. When they say something kind to you, they are not trying to accrue any favor with you; they are just plain thoughtful and generous.

I have never met Michael Jackson, but maybe, just maybe the same qualities that I see and love about young children, he saw in them also, and that's why he preferred their company. Everybody has the right to their own opinion, but I choose to believe that whenever it was possible, Mr. Jackson would seek refuge from a world that at times can be not so nice at times, in the unconditional, caring company of a child.

I hope that I am right and that history will be kind to Michael Joseph Jackson.

MOVING STAIRS

No matter where you go, there you are.

—*Buckaroo Banzai*

St. Louis, Missouri, was founded in 1764 by Pierre Laclede and Auguste Chouteau. In 1904, the city hosted the World's Fair and the Olympic Games. Over the course of the city's long and storied history it has always been considered an epicenter of commerce and travel. Every year, tourists visit St. Louis from all around the world, but primarily from the Midwest. We have people who travel to the city from southern Illinois, Arkansas, Nebraska, and Iowa.

One weekend at the hotel, I met three ladies and their preteen children who were visiting St. Louis from Kansas. They were going to be in town for only a few days, so while they were here, they visited Grant's Farm (home of the Clydesdale horses) on Thursday, Forest Park (the largest public park in the country) on Friday, and the St. Louis Zoo (the number three-rated zoo in the world) on Saturday. After a long day at the zoo, they put their kids to bed and then came down to the bar for a nightcap; they planned on driving home early Sunday morning. The ladies were well-educated, perceptive people. Two of them had master's degrees, and the third was currently working on her doctoral degree. Meeting and talking to them was both educational and refreshing. No subject matter was avoided, and none of us were politically correct.

They asked me where I was from. I told them that I was born and raised in East St. Louis, Illinois, but for the last twelve years I have lived in downtown St. Louis. One of the ladies inquired what it was like growing up and living in East St. Louis. They had heard that it was a rough and dangerous place. I told them it wasn't easy. East St. Louis has more than its fair share of crime, but what place doesn't have some degree of crime?

One of the ladies asked if there was a lot of crime in downtown St. Louis. I told them that in my opinion, there is no more than any major city in the world.

Another one of the ladies mentioned that upon entering the parking garage at the hotel, they noticed a yellow sign that reads "PARK SMART: Store Your Valuables out of Sight." What's up with that? I explained that there have been times when cars parked in the garage have been broken into, but not very often in comparison to other areas of the city.

I told them that for ten years I lived in the apartment building adjacent to the hotel, and knock on wood, at no time during my residency, was my car broken ever into. I now live in the area of town known as the Washington Loft District, and early in the summer of 2011 we were hit hard with a rash of car burglaries. The main strip near where I live is Washington Avenue. Every Saturday night, every available parking space on Washington Ave. and the nearby side streets is occupied by the vehicles of people who patronize the restaurants, bars, and nightclubs in and around the Washington Loft District. To my dismay, on many early Sunday mornings, while driving to work, I would pass streams of broken glass on the curb of both sides of my street, the origin of the glass being broken car windows, the result of smash and grab burglaries. *Smash and grab* is a term used to describe a two-person team of car burglars who break into motor vehicles and steal whatever is visible inside them. They just walk down a row of cars, one member of the team breaks out the car window, and the other member of the team, walking in lockstep right behind him, grabs whatever he can as quickly as possible. They move fast, walking from car to car, block to block, breaking into cars. To maximize the number of cars broken into, I suspect that there are multiple teams of smash and grab bandits working one street at a time, on different nights, hitting one area of town after another.

The downtown area is not the only place menaced by this plague of robberies. There are police reports of similar crimes occurring in the surrounding counties of St. Charles and Jefferson. In the fall of 2011, I noticed a drop in the number of car break-ins. Rumor has it, the police caught the culprits during a minor traffic stop, and allegedly they were driving a van full of stolen items. If the rumor about how they were apprehended is true, I personally am not sure why they would cruise around the city in a vehicle full of their stolen booty, but I have deduced from watching the local evening news that a lot of our local, small-time criminals are *not very smart*.

With a well-deserved sense of pride, one the ladies from Kansas, speaking for the group, told me that they have zero crime where they live. They live in a small community of twelve families about thirty minutes west of Kansas City. They are a close-knit community, everyone knows everybody, they are for the most part friends with each other, and at least pleasant acquaintances. They do not lock their car doors or their home doors. There is no need to; everyone where they live respects their neighbors' privacy and belongings. They home school their children until they are middle school age, then the kids bus to Kansas City, were they attend private school.

I told them that the way of life they described sounds utopian, and they are truly blessed.

One of the ladies asked, "Why do you think your car has never been broken into?"

I told them it's because I have *Crooktonite* on the front passenger seat of my car. I explained that Crooktonite is whatever book I'm reading at the time. The criminals don't want to steal a book. As a matter of fact, they run away screaming, "Nobody gonna make me read a book, *no way, no how!*" Judging by the confused look on the ladies faces, I don't think they understood the crux of my joke. I told them that I was just teasing, and that I believed the reason why my vehicle had not been broken into was a combination of luck and the fact that I never leave anything visible in my car worth taking. When a prospective car burglar looks in my car windows, all he sees is whatever book I'm reading at the time on the seat, nothing else. One of the ladies said she is so happy they don't have such problems where they live. Once again I told them that I considered them blessed, but I added that while they are here in St. Louis, they should do as the natives do: place all valuables out of sight in their vehicle, and lock their vehicle's doors.

When I arrived at work the next morning, from a distance, I saw the ladies from Kansas and their children standing near the hotel front desk. I headed toward them, intending to say good morning, and to thank them for the interesting conversation the night prior, and wish them a safe journey home. As I got closer, I noticed that one of the ladies was having an animated conversation with the hotel security guard, while the other ladies were tending to the kids, who appeared to be upset. Recognizing that something was definitely wrong and not wanting to interrupt, I detoured by them and proceeded to the bar.

About an hour later, one of the ladies from Kansas stopped by the bar and told me that in the early morning, ten vehicles in the garage had been broken into, one of them the van that they rented for their trip to St. Louis. They had not heeded my warning to return to the van and store everything out of sight or just remove what they couldn't hide and take it up to their room. She also admitted that they had not locked the van's doors either, though not out of disrespect for my sage advice. She honestly couldn't explain exactly why they didn't listen, but she wishes now they had done so. She added that the one silver lining, if anything positive could be taken from something as traumatizing as being the victim of a crime, was that because the van doors were unlocked, the crooks didn't break their windows. They ransacked the van, but it seems that as far as they could tell, nothing of value was taken.

At that moment, the rest of her group joined us at the bar. One of the other ladies said, "I guess you know what happened to us. I bet you think we're pretty dumb."

I told her, "Not at all." I explained, "I'm a firm believer that we as human beings have certain inalienable rights, one of them being free will. We have the right to make our own choices, and we make them based on our own relative knowledge. It's unrealistic to think that an hour talking to me would resonate with you to the point that it would cause you to change years of behavior. I try not to judge, because if I were to visit your neck of the woods, I would not start leaving my house or car door open just because you said it was safe, so how could I expect you to do anything different? I'm just happy nothing valuable was taken. I hope that negative incident doesn't taint your perception of St. Louis and its people."

One of the ladies assured me that it wouldn't. Other than the break-in, they had a wonderful time in St. Louis and will definitely visit again, but next time they will be more careful and respect the rules of the environment.

The fifth night we passed St. Louis, and it was like the whole world lit up. In St. Petersburg they use to say there was twenty to thirty thousand people in St. Louis, but I never believed it till I see that wonderful spread of lights at two o'clock that still night. There weren't a sound there; everybody was asleep.

—*The Adventures of Huckleberry Finn*

To be a successful bartender, you need to be knowledgeable about drink recipes, be able to perform your duties in a fast and proficient manner, and be hospitable. (No one wants to be served by a *jerk*.) In my humble opinion, the most important attribute of a good bartender is his or her communication skills. Depending on the setting, people come to the bar for a number of reasons. Sometimes getting a drink is last on the list. Most of the time, information is the number one reason people come to my bar. They ask questions like: "Where's a good place locally to eat?" "How far is the airport from here?" "Who's pitching for the Cardinals tonight?" "How do you get to the Arch?" Believe it or not, the most commonly asked question at my bar is, "Where are the restrooms?"

My bar is located on the street level, in the lobby of a hotel. There are no restrooms located on that level. The closest restroom is on the Promenade level, which is the next level above the street level. Guests can get to the Promenade level using the elevators or the escalator in the lobby. A bare minimum of five times a day, I give guests directions to the restrooms. I instruct them to take the escalator to the Promenade level, and then to proceed left, and they'll run into the restrooms on their left. Most of the time, guests have no problem finding the restrooms when given those directions, but often, once I'm finished giving the directions, the person receiving them appears to be confused. He'll walk away, head to the escalator and right by it, to places unknown, leaving me perplexed.

During a casual conversation with one of the hotel front desk agents, I mentioned this reoccurring phenomenon to her. She said she has given similar directions to guests, eliciting the same perplexed look and action, the only difference being they walk past the escalator and into the lobby instead of to places unknown. She added that she has experienced similar incidents when giving directions to the elevator. Inquirers usually head up the escalator, rather than take the elevator.

One day a gentleman who appeared to be a little intoxicated approached the bar and asked: "Where is the closest restroom?" I gave him directions, and he walked away—past the escalator. Later I found out he continued to the front desk and asked them for directions to the closest restroom. They gave him directions similar to mine. He walked back past the escalator to the bar and asked, "Can someone *please* point me to the nearest #*#** restroom!" Frustrated, I pointed to the escalator and told him, "*Go up the escalator. Once you reach the top, make a left. The restrooms are only a few feet away, on the left-hand side of the hallway!*" He then asked, "Do you mean the restrooms are up the *moving stairs?*" At that moment I understood; it hit me like a ton of bricks: He didn't know the proper name for the moving stairs is *escalator*; therefore, he was confused.

Ignoring the fact that he seemed intoxicated, if he didn't know *that*, maybe he's not alone; maybe other people who are confused with my directions don't know either, or maybe they get the two terms *escalator* and *elevator* mixed up. The people who headed off to places unknown, may have been confused and took the elevator, and vice versa for people who received directions from the front desk agent and took the escalator instead of the elevator. The lesson learned: It's not that people don't know the difference between an elevator and an escalator. Be cognizant of the reality that the people you are dispensing information to, through no fault of yours or their own, may not understand what you are telling them. If so, maybe if you explain it differently you'll get your point across.

In these tough economic times, when money is scarce, I make myself available to my employer, letting them know that I am always available if they need help in any capacity at the hotel. I want to work. Once, while filling in for the in-room dining attendant, I met a young couple in the elevator on my way to deliver a room service order. My hotel has six elevators, two of which have glass exteriors, giving the occupants a view of the city. During the trip to my destination, I exchanged greetings with the couple, and they asked a couple of questions about the ins and outs of how room service works. I did my best to answer all their questions. When I reached my destination floor, I wished them a good day, and let them know that if they had any further questions about in-room dining, not to hesitate to give us a call.

About ten minutes passed by the time I delivered my order and called another elevator. The first available elevator was the same glass elevator I was previously on. To my surprise, the same young couple I met earlier were on it. They still had their luggage. My first thought was, *Is this some* Ground Hog Day *type of experience?* But in seriousness I asked, "Is everything okay? Is there a problem with your room or something else?"

Appearing to be a little embarrassed, they told me that they had not been to their room yet. They had been riding the elevator up and down, enjoying the view. They were from a small town in Tennessee. St. Louis is the biggest city they have ever been to, and our hotel was the tallest building they had ever been in. Meeting that couple help me realize how I take for granted where I live, the places I have been, and the experiences I have had. Not everyone lives in a city where structures like the St. Louis Arch, buildings like One Metropolitan Square, and the Thomas F. Eagleton United States Courthouse are commonplace.

> A pessimist sees the difficulty in every opportunity; an optimist sees the opportunity in every difficulty.
>
> —*Winston Churchill*

When I was a young man, back in the day, I lived to go out to bars and nightclubs and party. Going out all the time, I became well-versed in certain bar etiquette. Tip the doorman, and he'll remember you; you will never have to wait in line to get in. On a busy night, be patient, and when the bartender gets to you, be ready to order and have your money ready to pay; and *always, always* tip the bartender. Never, ever piss the bartender off, because if you do, you can forget about getting another drink that night, and if you do get one, I wouldn't drink it.

Now that I am a bartender, it seems like every day I encounter more and more people who don't know any bar etiquette, or simply don't care about bar etiquette. If I had a dollar for every time someone has come to the bar and been rude to me or didn't know what they wanted to drink or weren't ready to pay when I served their drink, or did not tip me, I would be rich. Those people are lucky that Easy-E was not their bartender. (Beware of the Visine)

I got my first bartending job in May of 1996. That means I have worked in the bar business for over sixteen years. Up until recently, my biggest pet peeve was, when I approach a customer and ask what would they like to drink and they respond "I don't know," or "What do you have?" Worse yet, "Make me something I would like", that is the response I hate the most. *You are a total stranger. How the hell am I supposed to know what you like?*

Of course, this situation happens more often than not when the bar is really busy. So what I normally do is point out our beer, wine, and liquor display, ask the guest to look over what's available, and when they make their choice and are ready to order, to let me know, and I'll get them what they want right away. Then I move on to the next guest.

Usually, when I tell them that, they develop a confused and sometimes angry look on their face, and eventually, when I get back around to them, they begrudgingly order just a beer or rum and coke or something generic like that, and leave the bar dissatisfied. When this happens, I always feel bad, but what am I supposed to do? I'm not a mind reader or Negrodamus, and I have other guests who know what they want clamoring for drinks. Luckily—for hospitality's sake—one Sunday afternoon, the light bulb came on, and I figured out a manageable solution.

Sunday afternoons at the hotel are usually very slow and calm. The majority of the weekend hotel guests have checked out, and normally, new guests don't check in until after 3:00 p.m. During this time there are few to no visitors to the bar. To keep busy, I spend that time tidying up the lobby. As many supervisors would say, "If you have time to lean, you have time to clean."

On one of these Sunday afternoons, when the lobby was unusually quiet (the lobby music was turned low and the bar TVs were muted), I overheard a conversation between a group of twenty-some things riding the escalator down from the Promenade level to the lobby. The topic of their conversation was the liquor bottles on display at the bar. They marveled at the amount and the seemingly endless variety of different types of liquor bottles. They wondered aloud and bantered between them about what the different types of liquors are, what they taste like, and what types of drinks are made with them. Then it dawned on me that when people are confused and don't know what drinks to order for themselves, my telling them to just look at the liquors displayed at the bar and get back with me when they are ready to order is not helping them get a drink one bit. Just because I am a bartender with sixteen years of experience, and I know that Malibu is a coconut rum, that Kahlua is a coffee liqueur, and I know what are the most popular mixers used with gin and vodka does not mean the average visitor to the bar knows. And we don't even want to broach the subject of wines. I work with wine every day, have read *Wine for Dummies* twice, and I still have limited wine knowledge. That day I knew that I needed to discover a new approach to helping guests figure out their prospective drink orders.

To assist me in finding a drink of choice for the guest who is unsure about what cocktail they would enjoy, I apply the Marco Polo game to bartending. I ask them key questions about alcoholic beverages they have enjoyed in the past (Marco). Using their answers (Polo), if I am lucky, I can figure out what drink they would find acceptable. The Marco Polo style of bartending almost always works when dealing with guests who are novices when it comes to their drink of choice. But it is time-consuming and not always plausible, especially when the bar is busy, but it is a step in the right direction.

To be a good, successful bartender you have to work hard and continue to learn new things. It's not easy, but most things in life worth having are hard.

EXTENDED STAY

Each friend represents a world in us, a world possibly not born until they arrive, and it is only by this meeting that a new world is born.

—*Anais Nin*

A December 30, 2010 article by Ernest Dempsey on Digital Journal Reports stated that entering 2011, there were 1.5 million homeless people in the US. At last count, in January 2010, there were 1,305 homeless people in St. Louis, Missouri. Most commercial businesses in downtown St. Louis discourage homeless people from lingering in front, around, and inside their establishments. If a homeless person is discovered hanging out in a downtown hotel, he is kindly asked to leave by hotel staff or security. Even though it seems cold-hearted, it is necessary. A lot of the homeless engage in panhandling, so hotel staff and management do not allow them on hotel property as a preventive measure, to shield guests from potentially uncomfortable confrontations.

A couple of years ago I read a story by Malcolm Gladwell called "Million-Dollar Murray." The story gave me insight to the homeless problem in our country that I had never considered. After reading the story, my perception when it comes to the homeless had been forever altered. As far as I am concerned, as long as an occasional homeless visitor to the hotel is not causing any problem or harassing a hotel guest, I turn a blind eye to their presence.

Some of the homeless I have encountered enter the hotel to use the public restroom or to absorb the congenial atmosphere of the hotel for a few moments. Who am I to begrudge them a few minutes of escape from an otherwise harsh reality of not having a home and living on the street? Whenever possible, I do my best to avoid donning the black hat and being the dark-hearted villain who denies shelter to a poor soul on a rainy morning, a scorching hot afternoon, or a bitterly cold night. It saddens me that here in the United States, the greatest country in the world, we do not have a better course of action when it comes to helping the homeless, street urchins, and the disenfranchised get on their feet.

Once a convention, large group, or company decides on a destination city to host its planned event, usually a week, a month, and sometimes a year prior, they will conduct site visits in the destination city at multiple hotels in hopes of determining which facility can best accommodate their needs. A hotel site visit is a tour in an official capacity of a lead representative or an advance scout of a potential client that is considering booking rooms or banquet space at our hotel for an event or meeting. The site visit consists of a tour of the hotel, its rooms, outlets, and meeting and banquet spaces. The tour is conducted by the prospective hotel's assigned sales representative, who answers pertinent questions about the hotel before, during, and after the tour. At my hotel, a site visit always begins and ends in the hotel lobby. Normally, an hour prior to the site visit, the sales representative conducting the tour inspects the lobby to ensure its tidiness.

Prior to one of these site visits, I noticed a tall, disheveled, older man enter the lobby and sit down on one of the lobby couches. After a few minutes, the man kicked off his shoes and proceeded to lie down on the couch. By his appearance, I took him for a homeless man, but I wasn't sure; even though his hair was messy and his hygiene appeared to be suspect, his shabby clothes were clean. Also, I have never seen a homeless person come in, kick off his shoes, and lie down. Normally, they might sit down, use the restroom, or ask for a glass of water, but never, ever kick off their shoes and lie down on the furniture.

A few minutes later, one of the hotel sales reps entered the lobby and began inspecting it in preparation for the impending site visit. She noticed the man on the couch and asked me if he was a hotel guest. I told her I had no idea and that he had just recently come in. She went over to the couch, took a look at him, and came back to the bar. She told me that he was asleep and he looked like a *bum*. Then she called security.

Once security arrived, the guard and the sales rep roused the gentleman, told him that he was not welcome in the hotel and asked him to leave. In a loud voice, the gentleman responded, "*What do you mean I'm not welcome? The front desk agent told me to relax in the lobby until my room is ready!*" The gentleman then asked both of them to follow him to the front desk, so they could get to the bottom of this matter. Five minutes later the sales rep returned to the bar with the gentleman. With egg on her face, she introduced the gentleman to me as Mr. Newton, told me that we were happy to have him as a guest, and that he could have any food or drinks he wanted for the rest of the day on the house. She then apologize to Mr. Newton for the misunderstanding earlier, gave him one of her business cards, and told him that if there was anything she could do to enhance his stay, to please let her know. I later learned that the gentleman had walked in, paid for four weeks (as Randy Moss would say, "Straight cash, homie!") to stay in one of the hotel suites, and was told to relax in the lobby until his accommodations were ready.

During Mr. Newton's stay at the hotel, he would spend hours at a time at the bar. Despite my attempts to strike up a conversation with him, he would not talk to me; the only interaction between the two us was he asking for a drink and me making and selling him said drink. He would sit near me at the bar and hold in-depth conversations with his imaginary friend *Saul*. The only person who could see, hear, and talk to Saul was Mr. Newton. Eavesdropping on their conversation, I determined that Mr. Newton is a staunch conservative, and in the words of Mr. Newton, Saul is a bleeding heart, left-wing Liberal Socialist. Mr. Newton hates President Obama, he is a homophobe (in his words, "God made Adam and Eve, not Adam and Steve"), and he believes that trickle down economics can bring the US out of this recession, among other things. Saul, on the other hand, denies adamantly that he is a Socialist, he loves Obama, he doesn't care who people choose to love (the more love on this planet, the better), and he thinks that it was proven during George W. Bush's presidential term that trickledown economics doesn't work.

Listening to Mr. Newton banter back and forth with his imaginary friend Saul was peculiar to say the least. Sometimes Mr. Newton would get loud and agitated, but I didn't mind. Most of the time, he and Saul were the only people at the bar and in the lobby. So it was no big deal; in my opinion, he was harmless.

One afternoon, I had two female guests having lunch at the bar. Like clockwork, Mr. Newton showed up and started talking to Saul. I subtly assured the ladies that he was a guest of the hotel and that even though he was strange, he posed no threat to them, me, or himself. Despite their best efforts, the ladies could not help but stare at Mr. Newton while he talked to Saul. Not appreciating the added solicitous attention from the ladies, Mr. Newton became agitated and asked Saul aloud, "What are those b*tches lookin' at?" The ladies heard what he said and were appalled. They insisted that I call someone in authority immediately. After the manager on duty arrived, a heated argument ensued involving the two female guests, the hotel manager, and Mr. Newton, with Saul doing his best to be the voice of reason and to calm Mr. Newton down. When the smoke cleared, the ladies' lunch was complimentary, and Mr. Newton was asked to leave the bar. An incensed Mr. Newton, with Saul in tow, left the bar, vacated his hotel room, and left the premises never to be seen again

The following paragraph is a brief synopsis of one of a couple of sub-plots in a 1980 movie called *Melvin and Howard*.

On a late night, a young man driving down US highway 95 in the Nevada desert pulls over to the side of the road to relieve himself. To his shock, he finds an injured old man who had been in a motorcycle accident. Being a Good Samaritan, he offers to take the injured man to a hospital. The injured man refuses to go to the hospital, but asks for a ride to Las Vegas. The young man obliges and gives him a ride. During the trip, the two engage in small talk, and a level of bonding occurs. The young man drops the old gentleman off at the Sands hotel in Vegas. Before parting ways, the old man tells the young man that he is Howard Hughes. Some time passes, and the young man receives a disputed hand-written will written by Howard Hughes leaving the young man 156 million dollars.

A month after I last saw Mr. Newton, I was out having dinner with an old friend who is an investment banker. I told him all about my encounter with Mr. Newton. He instantly recognized the name. It turns out Mr. Newton is a wealthy ex-stockbroker who retired a few years ago. He described Mr. Newton as having a keen mind and being a savvy businessman. When his wife passed away three years ago, he seems to have lost it. He retired, sold their home, and has been living in hotels all around the city. *Saul* was the name of his best friend since childhood, who died about five years ago. Mr. Newton's picture should be the illustration next to saying, "Never judge a book by its cover."

For the last four-plus years, I have worked an average of 320 days each of those years. I work my normal workweek, which is normally four or five shifts. On my days off, my supervisors know that I am available if any other shifts need to be filled. When business dictates the need for added manpower, I volunteer. If one of my co-workers asks me to work a shift for them I accept. If someone calls in sick or is a *no-show, no-calls* I report to work to cover the shift. I work a lot because I suffer from what my mother calls "beer pockets and champagne taste." My grandmother taught me that if you work hard, you can have whatever you desire. So I choose to change my pockets, rather than my taste.

My work schedule is possible because I am single (I'm a loser), and I don't have any children. Since I am at work most of the time, I am seldom at my own residence. The hotel has become my home, and my co-workers have become a surrogate family to me. The restaurant staff (Carlos, Tasha, Willie, and the others) are my pseudo-cousins. Two of my bartending peers (Martez and Julie) are like my little brother and sister. Last but not least, to complete our little cabal, we have the matriarch of the bar, the cantankerous one herself, Donna. I consider these people to be just as much my family as I do my real family. We don't always agree with each other and get along. We fight and argue often, but at the end of the day, we love each other. God help the outsider who disrespects or crosses one of us.

A year ago, we had an unsolicited addition to our hotel family: Mr. Fredrick Walter Lockett, who introduces himself as F. W. for short. Mr. Lockett's role in our family is that of a distant cousin who came to visit, but never left. Mr. Lockett moved to St. Louis to be close to his son, who had recently graduated from Duke University with a bachelor's degree and was now attending Washington University in St. Louis to pursue his master's degree. Mr. Lockett's plan was to stay at a hotel while looking for a suitable permanent residence. His plan had stalled because he fell in love with the convenient location of our hotel when it comes to proximity to local activities, restaurants, stores, and other downtown amenities. He was finding it most difficult to find reasonably priced lodging elsewhere that offers the same creature comforts, so for all intents and purposes, he has lived in our hotel for a year plus.

During Mr. Lockett's residency at our hotel, he has used all of the hotel's amenities and outlets. Every day, he has lunch, dinner, and cocktails at the bar. Because of the frequency of his bar visits, I have gotten to know Mr. Lockett quite well; he is an interesting character, who has lived a colorful life.

If I had to choose one word to describe him, that word would be *entertainer*. Mr. Lockett is an accomplished thespian; he once had a role in an off Broadway production of *Death of a Salesman*. He is also a classically trained pianist. At one point in his life he worked as a session musician at the legendary Sun Records Studio. He has met and worked with Elvis Presley, the Neville Brothers, and Jim Belushi and the Blues Band, just to name a few. Listening to Mr. Lockett recount his experiences, I become a captive, enamored listener. His appearance reminds me of Don Quixote of La Mancha. The fictional Don Quixote fantasized that windmills were dragons that he tried to slay. Mr. Lockett's dragons are the obstacles that life throws at him. Throughout his life, whenever he was given lemons, he made lemonade. Mr. Lockett has a wealth of knowledge and experiences that overflow; whenever I need advice, he is always a willing benefactor.

Mr. Lockett is always encouraging me not to be so formal, and to address him as F. W. or Fred. As he puts it, "We are friends and friends are normally on first name basis." I usually accommodate his request and address him as F. W. when he mentions it, but by the time our next encounter rolls around, I usually revert back to referring to him as Mr. Lockett. I agree with Mr. Lockett, we do have a nascent friendship, but because he is a guest of the hotel, I am apprehensive about taking liberties and not remaining professional. My reluctance is founded in the fear that over time our relationship will evolve one of two ways: we will become good friends, or familiarity will breed contempt. It's inevitable that as people continue to get to know each other over an extended time, they start to notice qualities they like and don't like about each other. As they learn more and more things they like about the other the friendship grows. As they learn more things they don't like about each other, animosity develop. What if over time I start to learn things about Mr. Lockett I don't like, or vice versa, he discovers things about me he doesn't like? If we were social friends and our friendship turned sour, we would just cease hanging out together, but since he lives where I work, it could lead to an uncomfortable situation for both of us. That is the dichotomy of workplace relationships, which are compounded when the friend is a constant customer. That is why I continue to refer to F. W. as Mr. Lockett, trying my best to maintain a professional environment. I would rather continue the status quo, than risk a possible negative outcome.

I know it is inevitable that the day will come when the hotel and I will part ways, whether because my services will no longer be required, or I move on to bigger and better things. Or the day will come when Mr. Lockett will discover his elusive comfortable lodging at an apartment or a house of his own. Until one of those two outcomes comes to fruition, I will continue to be the bartender first and foremost, and do my part to ensure he has an awesome experience at our hotel. "Hello Mr. Lockett, welcome to the bar. Would you like to take a look at menu or is it time for a *real* drink?"

PART 3

GRATUITY

AN HONEST QUESTION

Make sure your soul's all right Cuz money didn't matter yesterday,
And it sure don't matter tonight.
—Prince Rodgers Nelson

M y mother loves to listen to morning talk radio shows. One day the topic was tipping at restaurants and bars. After the show ended, she had some questions about tipping, and who better to ask than her son who works at a bar? She called me up and gave me a brief rundown of the show, and then asked her number one question, "Why are people required to tip?"

I tried to explain to her that tipping is not mandatory, merely a form of etiquette that exists in the service industry. A tip is known as a *gratuity*, a way of thanking your server, bartender, or whoever renders you service for doing a good job.

She responded, "Why should I give them money for doing a good job? When I go to a restaurant or bar I pay for my food and drinks, and the owners hire and pay employees to serve and take care of the guests who patronize their establishments. Why should I then turn around and give that employee more money on top of what they are already being paid, for doing what they are already supposed to be doing anyway?"

I tried to no avail to explain to her that it's hospitality etiquette to tip when you have been given good service, and that if the service is average or below average, people usually don't tip. I also explained to her that a lot of people who are servers or bartenders don't get paid even minimum wage, that because they are considered *tipped* employees, they get below minimum wage. (The minimum amount employers can pay tipped employees varies from state to state. Here in Missouri, tipped employee minimum wage is $3.625 an hour.) So the gratuity you leave them for services rendered helps those people make ends meet, and to take care of themselves and their families.

After quietly listening to my rationale for why people should tip, she still had the same question: "*Why should people have to tip?*"

Being the staunch supporter of tipping that I am, I got *pissed off and frustrated* with her and responded, "Look, around your home, most of the *shit* in your place was bought by me. Where do you think the money that paid for that stuff came from? *Tips!*" Then I hung up on her. The next day I called and apologized, and we both agreed that the subject of tipping was just something we would never see eye-to-eye on and to just leave it at that.

My mother is not alone in our society when it comes to people's stance on the practice known as tipping. A lot of people share her belief: *Why should I tip someone for doing the job that they are already being paid to do?* Then you have the people who believe tipping is just like taking your next breath: involuntary, an ingrained part of your restaurant, bar, or social experience.

What is up with this tipping business anyway?

A *tip* (also called a *gratuity*) is a voluntary extra payment made to certain service sector workers in addition to the advertised price of the transaction. Such payments and their size are a matter of social custom. Tipping varies among cultures and by service industry. Though by definition a tip is never legally required, and its amount is at the discretion of the patron being served, in some circumstances, failing to give an adequate tip when one is expected is a serious faux pas, and may be considered very miserly, a violation of etiquette, or unethical. In some other cultures or situations, giving a tip is not expected, and offering one would be considered at best odd or at worst condescending or demeaning. In some circumstances, such as with US government workers, receiving tips is illegal. Some restaurants implement a mandatory tip for dining parties of six or more people.

According to the Oxford English Dictionary:

> the word *tip* originated as a slang term, and its etymology is unclear. The term in the sense "to give a gratuity" first appeared in the eighteenth century. It derived from an earlier sense of *tip*, meaning "to give; to hand, to pass," which originated in the Rogues' cant [the secret language of criminals] in the seventeenth century.

Most bartenders don't like cheap tippers, but they *hate* non-tippers. Thus the level of hospitality and customer service they give to those labeled bad or non-tippers is subpar at best.

Through time, life experiences, and because it's just not in my nature to hate anyone, my perception of non-tippers has softened. No matter what your profession, you need to maintain a high level of professionalism, do a good job, and let karma take care of the rest. Don't get me wrong: I'm not a saint; I personally have a problem with people who work for tips (tipped employees in the service industry) but who are bad tippers themselves, or worse yet, don't tip at all. I think it's a huge oxymoron to work for tips, but when you go out, you don't tip; that's crazy to me. To give those people good service, and not get pissed at them when they don't take care of you, is a work in progress for me, but I am trying.

What's considered a *good* tip?

What's a *good* tip? I have to be honest; I don't know the answer to that question. I do know that nothing at all is bad. I have found that a tip can vary from a monetary amount to gifts (big, small to inexpensive, to the very expensive, to even stock tips). What bartenders consider to be a good tip to be is based on the standard they have personally set for themselves. That standard can be based on what they have experienced, observed, earning goals they have set, or all of the above. I can't speak for all bartenders, so I'll just give my personal opinion on a starting point: an average tip is 15 percent of your total bill; an above-average tip is 25 percent of your total bill; a great tip is 33 percent of the bill; and an *awesome* tip is 50 percent or more of the total bill.

My Daddy

The bar is busy. People are lined up at the bar. Some are yelling out for drinks, and others are waving money at me, hoping to get my attention. I'm doing my best to take care of everyone in a timely manner. I look up and notice him walk in. I get excited, stop making drinks, wave to him, and he acknowledges me. It's him; it's *my Daddy*.

No, he is not my father; I just refer to him as my Daddy. I think of him in this way, because when he comes in, I get excited like a small child would when his father comes home with a new toy for him. Instead of a toy, his being there guarantees me a bare minimum of fifty dollars in tips. He is my best-tipping customer. He moves toward the busy bar, I yell out, "The usual," he gives me the thumbs up, the people who have been waiting, who where there before him, start getting restless. I pass his drink to him and ask, "Shall I start you a tab?" He nods okay. Now I ask, "Whose next?" *What the hell just happened?* Is the consensus feeling among all the patrons at the bar?

This scenario probably happens pretty often at bars around the world. In the bar business, *good* tippers get preferential treatment. Is it right? Yes or no—it all depends on your perspective. Sometimes though, it works against a customer to be recognized as a good tipper, because sometimes your good will is taken for granted (he always tips no matter what), thus the level of prompt good service isn't always what it should be.

RIP Lew Korsmeyer.

You can keep your quarters

Just because a patron is a good tipper doesn't necessarily mean he is a good person. I have personally gotten great tips from people who for the most part have been assholes, nutjobs, or creeps. I have had customers justify not tipping me, whether consciously or subconsciously, for a number of reasons: because I didn't put enough alcohol in their drink; because I didn't put a garnish on their drink; because I didn't get to them and take their order fast enough; because I didn't put a napkin down first; and there is my personal favorite excuse: "I don't tip men." And there are some people who walk on tabs in hopes of avoiding having to tip. (A lot of bars post signage stating that a 20 percent gratuity will be added to all walk-out tabs), and some people just plain honestly forget.

I want to state for the record that we should never confuse a bad tipper with a bad person; the two are totally different. Just because a person doesn't tip you, you can't consider him *bad, evil,* or *ungrateful.*

There could be a number of reasons why a person doesn't tip. Believe it or not, some people don't know that they *should* tip. Maybe it's their first time in a bar, or maybe they have never worked in a hospitality setting, so they don't know the etiquette. We also have to accept the fact that some people can't afford to tip. If they tip us, they can't buy as many drinks as they want, or they will not have enough money to buy something to eat on the way home. A lot of bartenders feel that people who can't afford to tip should just stay home. I personally will not go anywhere if I can't afford to tip, but that doesn't mean that people who don't share my point of view should stay home.

> Blessed is he who expects nothing, for he shall never be disappointed.
>
> —*Alexander Pope*

Once I was working an extremely slow day shift. It was pretty dismal. A guy came in and ordered a domestic beer. I got the beer for him and told him that it would be $4.50. He gave me five dollars and said, "Keep the change." I thanked him and wished him a good day.

He interpreted my response as sarcasm and told me so. I quickly explained to him that I meant no disrespect, that my thank-you was sincere, and that my grandmother taught me to always say thank you when given anything. I explained that I understand that he didn't have to give me anything, and that I truly appreciate any and all tips.

A week later, the same guy came in, ordered a beer, and gave me a ten-dollar tip. He explained that the week prior he was running short on money, having a bad day, and just wanted to stop off on the way home to have a beer and relax. He wanted me to know that he appreciated my kindness and service the week before.

At first I didn't even remember him, and then I thought to myself it was cool that he remembered me from the week earlier and took care of me this time around. Honestly, at the time of our first encounter, all I remember is that it was a slow day, and my only intent was to do a good job and give good service. I had no idea that he would ever be back, or if he did come back, that he would be so generous.

That day was a turning point in my career as a bartender. I learned one of the most valuable lessons of my bartending career: Always treat people the way we would like to be treated, and don't worry whether they tip us. Stay classy, be a good person, always be professional, and things will work out for you in the long run.

I can spot a *good* tipper a mile away

Back in 1992, my roommate at the time was Chris, a good-looking, snazzy-dressing, charismatic, good guy. He worked as a cell phone salesman back in the infancy of cell phones, when there were very few cell phone stores, and Chris's cell phone store was his briefcase. This is when cell phones cost anywhere from seven hundred to a thousand dollars.

Chris would go to people's homes and sell them a phone in their living room. He wore a suit virtually all day, every day; he never knew when a lead would pop up, so he had to always be ready to make a sale. Chris would go anywhere and sell phones to anyone. A lot of his customers would pay him for phones in cash, so sometimes Chris would have thousands of dollars in cash on him.

When Chris went to bars, he would get elite service. He would order a soda, then reach in his pocket and peel through hundreds, fifties, and twenties, and then pay for his drink. The bartenders would be salivating with anticipation as they handed him his change, and he would leave them an average tip. To say that the bartenders were disappointed is definitely an understatement. In defense of Chris: He is a very generous man, but the reality of the situation was he couldn't afford an above-average tip. Sales were few and far between, so at times he made very little in commissions. So if the bartenders assumed he was a good tipper because of the way he was dressed, the clothes he had on were literally his work uniform. If the bartenders thought he would be a great tipper because of the money he flashed, the money he had on him wasn't his to spend, and definitely not his to tip. If the bartenders hoped he would take care of them because he was a nice guy, sometimes nice guys just don't have money to give.

In speaking about Chris, my intent is definitely not to defame him. Chris was one of my closest and dearest friends. What I want everyone to understand is that you can't determine if someone is a good tipper by the way he looks, the clothes he wears, the money he has, or his personality. I have worked in the bar business off and on for the past sixteen years, and I can proudly say that I have been tipped generously and not tipped at all, by people from all walks of life. Regarding tipping or not tipping, gender, age, race, nationality, rich, poor ... there is no absolute science when it comes to the tipping game. There is no secret formula that exists to help you make money as a bartender. I believe in karma; I always tell new bartenders to put all their energies into doing a good job, and they will be successful. I try to point out to them that success is not always measured monetarily.

The *best* tips I have *ever* received

Recently, I had a job at a bar located in a hotel lobby. My boss loved the smell of freshly popped popcorn. He feels the smell is inviting (and he is right). So every day for happy hour the bartender on duty would pop fresh popcorn at the bar, and true to form, the smell would fill the lobby and entice guests to partake of the complimentary snack, and sometimes buy a drink from the bar also.

One day while I was getting ready to pop the popcorn, I noticed a family in the lobby waiting to check into their room. It was a woman and two young girls. (I guessed their ages to be between six and eight.) They caught my attention because of the unrelenting, curious stare of the girls while I prepped the popcorn machine; they seemed so intrigued by every part of the process of popping the popcorn. After the popcorn was ready, I grabbed a couple of baskets, filled them with popcorn, approached the family, and said, "Hello, my name is Celester, and how are you guys doing today?" I then asked the adult if it was okay to give the girls the popcorn.

The woman said, "Thank you that is very kind of you."

I said, "No problem. Hello young ladies, this is for you."

They didn't say a word; they just looked at me with an expression of *awe* on their faces. I don't know if I mentioned this: I am six feet four inches and weigh 250 pounds, and this is the general reaction I get from small children. As my girlfriend at the time would say, tongue-in-cheek, "You are a monster." They looked at each other and then back at me and took the baskets of popcorn.

The woman with them said, "What do you say to the nice man?"

The girls in chorus said, "Thank you."

I responded, "You are very welcome, and you guys have a good day," and went back to work at the bar.

An hour later, the woman and the two little girls came up to the bar and patiently waited to get my attention. Curious, I approached them and asked, "What's going on, guys? Is there something I can get for you?"

The woman said, "No, we're fine. The girls have something for you, though."

The girls pulled two flowers from behind their backs and handed them to me. You could have knocked me over with a feather; I thought that was so sweet. I thanked them and they said, "You are very welcome. Goodbye." I put the flowers in a cup of water and proudly displayed them at the bar for the rest of the day.

Later I saw one of our hotel managers pacing on the adjacent patio, it seemed like something was wrong. I went up to her and asked, "What's going on? You seem frustrated."

She replied, "I don't know who or why, but someone has taken all our flowers off the patio trees."

On another occasion, I served lunch to a couple and their five-year-old daughter. While waiting for their food to be prepared, I was standing at the bar talking to another guest, when the little girl walked up to the bar and asked if I had any crayons. When I told her I didn't have any, her face dropped; she looked so sad. Then I remembered that I had seen crayons in the restaurant's hostess stand. I told the little girl I had an idea where I could get some, and that I would bring them to her table when I found them. So I went to the restaurant, got the crayons, and brought them to her. She was so excited; she kept saying, "Thank you, thank you, thank you!"

After finishing their meal and before they left, the little girl came up to the bar again. I said, "Hello my little friend."

She responded, "Hello, this is for you," and handed me the picture she had colored.

I was again taken back, I told her, "Thank you so much." The guest at the bar who had been privy to the whole situation suggested that I have her sign the picture. I asked the little girl if she would sign her name to the picture, and she graciously obliged.

She ran off and joined her parents as they were leaving, but before they left the lobby, she turned and said, "Goodbye, see you later." As they left, the guests sitting at the bar commented on how nice the whole interaction was. I agreed as I looked at my picture she had given me, signed *Abby*.

More than just a grand slam

I don't go out to bars very often (I'm getting old), but when I do go out, I normally start a tab and tip anywhere between 25 to 33 percent, except when I'm buzzed, or as my friend Paul would poke fun at me and say, "I turn into Sebastian Rockefeller." Then I usually tip 50 percent and above. I am by no means rich; it's just that I'm in the bar business, and am a firm believer in my own credo: "How can you expect to receive a good tip if you are not willing to give one?"

Even before I was in the bar business, I understood the etiquette of tipping. I was taught Tipping 101 by an old roommate's wife, Victoria, who once worked as a server at Denny's. She worked the graveyard shift (11:00 p.m. to 6:00 a.m.). In my opinion, a server working the graveyard shift at Denny's has the hardest job in hospitality. To anyone who has ever eaten at Denny's between the hours of 1:00 a.m. and 6:00 a.m., I ask you to close your eyes, take a moment, and imagine yourself in the server's shoes. Its 3:00 a.m. on a Friday or Saturday night, the nightclubs in your area have just closed, and their drunk, loud, belligerent patrons are now your guests. They are impatient, unreasonable, demanding, and have a drunken sense of right and wrong. You patiently take their orders, you rush to get their food, and you work hard to take care of them. All the while, they are unrelentingly critical of every aspect of their dining experience. No matter what you do, they are never quite satisfied. They finish their meal, you present the check, they pay, and guess what—no tip, or what I consider worse, an insultingly low tip. Now, does that scenario happen all the time? No, but it does happen more than it should. That was an example of an average weekend shift for Victoria.

She hasn't worked as a server for years, but whenever we would go to Denny's, she would make us leave a 100 percent tip. She had a ritual: we would pay at the counter, go place the tip on the table, and then hurry outside. She would hide in the shadows, look through the window, and observe the server while she collects her tip from the table. Initially, I thought her behavior was strange, but because of a situation I later observed, I experienced a change of heart. Victoria's husband and I were waiting in the car for her like we always had, but this time it was taking her longer than usual to finish her tip ritual. So we went to check on her, there she was, crouched down in the shadows, looking through the window with a smile from ear to ear. She asked us to look at the server as she approached our vacated table.

The server started to clear the table. She noticed the money, picked it up, and started to count it. As she counted, a look of surprise was written all over her face. She started to look around as if she were looking for us; we were nowhere to be found. The server covered her face and started to weep. I looked at Victoria and she was crying also. Why was the server crying? Was it the amount, the thought behind it, or both? Why was Victoria crying? Who knows why the server cried? Maybe that tip enabled her to pay a crucial bill that was overdue. Maybe that was the only tip she received all night. Maybe the substantial amount indicated a level of appreciation that she had never received. I don't know; all I do know is on that occasion we were instrumental in brightening someone's day.

Recently, I started tipping a couple of bucks when I go to Subway and when I go through the drive-through at fast food restaurants. You would not believe how happy and appreciative those people are, at least after they get over the initial *shock* that I or anyone would tip them. Through them I have been able to get a better understanding of how Victoria and the server felt that now-distant night at Denny's. In my mind, in some situations a sincere thank-you is great, but when you add a monetary tip, it's like adding an exclamation point, and that makes that thank-you scream out, "*I appreciate you!*"

EPILOGUE

My Brother's Keeper

> God doesn't care who you were. He only cares who you are.
> —*Cowboys and Aliens*

I *H-A-T-E* to drive! The only thing I loathe more than driving is doing a leg workout at the gym. The problem is that I cannot go without doing either of the two things I profess to despise the most. I cannot imagine not having a car, because I love the freedom of having my own vehicle and being able to go where I please whenever I want. I have to do a leg workout at least once a week, because like most people who are training or working out, I desire to achieve and maintain a symmetrical build. (I cannot stand those chicken legs.) I'll do almost anything to avoid getting behind the wheel of a car.

I have a tremendous amount of anxiety when it comes to driving. I am always worried about getting into an accident, whether it's me hitting another vehicle, another vehicle hitting me, or me hitting a pedestrian.

For years I lived in an apartment that was only a couple of blocks away from the hotel I worked at. It was perfect. I walked to and from work and drove only when it was absolutely necessary. I saved money on gas, kept the mileage on my vehicle low, and avoided wear and tear on the vehicle. In 2009 I bought a loft. Proximity to my job was a major factor when it came to choosing my home. I was very lucky to find a place that I really liked, just a ten—to fifteen-minute drive to work. The bulk of my journey takes place on Olive Street, which runs eastbound through the heart of the city. My journey on Olive begins at Tucker Street and spans eight blocks to Fourth Street. Olive is a metropolitan street littered with high-rise office buildings, banks, restaurants, lofts, convenience stores, a post office, a grocery store, and other businesses. Driving on Olive has not only increased my driving anxiety, but it has increased my exasperation with all forms of traffic.

Traffic is defined as the passage of people or vehicles along routes of transportation. During rush hour or lunchtime, the main sources of traffic on Olive are pedestrians, bicycle riders, and motor vehicles, both personal and commercial. There are traffic laws that govern traffic and regulate vehicles, and there are rules of the road, which are both the laws and the informal rules that have developed over time to facilitate the orderly and timely flow of traffic. For pedestrians, the generally accepted rule of the road is that they have the right of way when crossing the road at crosswalks, but most of my city's pedestrians have taken that rule a step further. The days are few and far between that I haven't observed a pedestrian cross the street in the middle of traffic or step out from between parked cars into a busy street. Most of these people are simply not paying attention to their surroundings. I attribute most of this behavior to the use of cell phones, headphones, and ear buds. On January 16, 2012, the Los Angeles Times did an article about how accidents have recently tripled involving pedestrians wearing headphones or ear buds and motor vehicles. While driving, I have embraced the saying, "I am my brother's keeper," because despite my annoyance, the general rule is that me being the driver, I have the responsibility, no matter who is at fault, to avoid a collision with a pedestrian.

Years ago, there used to be a commercial on TV that had an elderly couple driving down the interstate, the lady is driving about thirty miles an hour, cars are zipping buy them, and all the while her husband is yelling at her, "Slow down! You're driving like a bat outta hell!" Some of my friends would say that I drive like the old lady, with the old man's perspective. While driving down Olive, not one day would pass without a car drifting into my lane and almost hitting me, a car driving too fast behind me, or the car ahead of me is driving too slow, from my perspective.

Another rule of the road is that traffic lights and stop signs should always be obeyed. A lot of my fellow drivers did not get that memo. Not a day goes by where I don't notice a driver either coast through a stop sign or red traffic light without making a complete stop, or just run through it all together.

On one occasion a car ran a red light and almost hit me. I was *pissed*. I exchanged a few bad words with the driver of the other car and then continued on my way. As I was driving on toward my destination, I noticed that the car that almost hit me was now following me. The car followed me up until I entered the parking garage at my job. I wasn't thinking straight: I parked, got out of my car, and went out to the garage entrance to challenge the driver; he had already left by the time I got there.

A week later, I told my friend Bud about what happened. He was a combination of angry, concerned, and disappointed. He angrily asked me, "Why did you get so mad at the other driver and participate in unnecessary, negative banter with him, especially considering that the accident was averted?" Then he asked, "What were you thinking when you parked your car and then went out looking to confront this possible *psychopath* after he followed you to work?" Before I could answer, he told me how stupid I was, and if the other driver had a weapon, I could have been hurt or killed.

Bud took a deep breath and calmed down. He apologized for calling me stupid and said he was happy that nothing bad happened and that I was okay. He told me that he thinks that I am a nice man, with a good heart; that's why this road rage incident seemed so out of character for me. He suggested that I should stop rationalizing my behavior based on the other guy's actions, but instead take a long, hard look at myself, because he believes the road rage incident is just a symptom of a much bigger, possibly festering problem within me.

Initially I was peeved by what I perceived to be Bud's demeaning rhetoric, but despite my hurt feelings, Bud's message was not lost in translation. Over the next couple of days, I went over and over it again in my head: the road rage incident and Bud's sharp rebuttal of said incident, and I came to realize that Bud was right. I accept the fact that the road rage incident was not totally the other driver's fault. I accepted the fact that I needed to take ownership of my role in the incident and acknowledge that if I had not reacted the way I did when the other driver ran the red light, most likely the situation would not have become so volatile. I recognized that I needed to make some adjustments in my behavior to make sure that an incident like the road rage incident or something even worse never happens again. I was aware that true change wasn't going to be easy, and it wasn't going to happen overnight, but I was determined to do what it took to make it happen.

I love discovering new words, learning what they mean, adding them to my vocabulary, and using them at the appropriate time. The same goes for quotes by famous, successful, influential people, past or present. Vince Lombardi was a Hall of Fame football coach for the Green Bay Packers; one of his famous quotes is, "If you're fifteen minutes early, you'll never be late." That quote is relevant to me; after much deliberation I felt that sentence would be the answer to helping me with some of my driving anxiety. You see, one of my pet peeves is that I hate being late for anything: for work, an appointment, or a date. Even though I hate being late, I seemed to find myself running behind and coming close to being late more often than I would like to admit.

The reasons for my frequent "almost tardiness" vary day to day. Sometimes I hit the snooze button more than I should instead of getting up right away when the alarm goes off. Sometimes I'm disorganized, and I can be literally halfway to my destination and realize I've forgotten something that is important and have to return home to retrieve it. Sometimes I simply run into some unforeseen obstruction such as traffic, road construction, or trouble finding a parking spot. I have found that if I apply a little self-discipline and begin my journey fifteen minutes or more earlier, it doesn't matter if the car ahead of me is going too slow to suit me, or if a pedestrian impedes my progress by walking out in front of traffic, or any unforeseen obstruction occurs; I can manage it and still arrive at my destination on time. Since I've been starting my journeys off earlier, my driving anxiety has definitely decreased, but not totally disappeared. Leaving earlier is a step in the right direction, but I still need to work hard at changing other aspects of my life for the better.

Recently, a friend posted the following statement on her Facebook wall:

So I was robbed at my car last night at gunpoint. Though shaken, I was physically unscathed and grateful for my life. Rather than spreading anymore anger or hate in this world, it is my wish that anyone reading this take a moment to send out a wave of love and hope through meditation, prayer, chanting, whatever your preference may be, to all of the people out there who are desperate enough, or sad enough, or hopeless enough to do something like this. May they have a change of heart and transition into decent human beings? And also, maybe you should get some mace just in case.

I have known the lady who was involved in that scary incident for at least 12 twelve years. She is one of the most easygoing, open-minded people I have ever met, and she is a rare breed who is a beautiful lady inside and out. Because of her uncanny ability to see the positive in any situation, she has always been a role model to me, but after reading that post she became an inspiration too.

I spend most of my free time engaged in deep thought, trying to figure out how I can improve and be a better person. Recently I heard a thought-provoking quote by Blaise Pascal, a seventeenth-century philosopher: "We are only truly happy when daydreaming about future happiness." After hearing that quote, I wanted to learn more about Pascal and read more of his work, so in a rush I went online and purchased the first book I came across with Pascal's name in the title. When I received the book, it wasn't exactly what I wanted. Instead of a book by Pascal, I received *Making Sense of It All: Pascal and the Meaning of Life* by Thomas V. Morris, a modern day philosopher. Mr.

Thomas's book was his interpretation of the *Pensées*. To say I was initially disappointed would be putting it mildly. I wanted to send it back, but I made the mistake of throwing away the receipt, and I knew trying to return it without the receipt would be a hassle that I did not have the stamina for. The book served as a paperweight for a month before I decided to read it. When I finally did give the book a chance and read it, the book turned out to be life-altering. It took me over a year to read it, because it had a lot of big words in it that I didn't know, and sometimes I would have to read parts of it over and over again before I could comprehend what I was reading.

In the Epilogue of my upcoming book, *Impromptu*, I go into more depth about the effect *Making Sense of it All* had on me, but for now there is one thing that I read in the book that is relevant to this story. Paraphrasing Mr. Thomas, 'You cannot expect a total stranger, who you never met, who has taken a totally different path, to get to this exact point of encounter, to have the same point of view as you.' That statement was a "Eureka moment" for me. I suddenly understood what my bigger issue that Bud hinted at was. I understood why I got so mad so often at people I met, observed, or passed daily. I perceived that there are universally accepted ideals of what is right and what is wrong that everyone should know and abide by.

Reading that statement opened my mind up to the possibility that the rules people live by are based on their environment and the life experiences they have been exposed to. So in short, what's right, what's wrong, rules, and personal etiquette are understood differently by each individual. I automatically assumed that when people did something wrong (from my point of view) that they just didn't care, or they were just indifferent. I read that statement over and over again to myself, and all I could think about is how arrogant and wrong I was for judging people based solely on my own point of reference. I was ashamed of myself and of all my past and recent behavior, but I was also encouraged, because then I understood what my issues were, and I could henceforth address them and start working on personal change.

What started off as an earnest attempt to relieve some driver's anxiety has evolved into a snowball of change rolling through my soul, getting bigger and bigger as it rolls downhill from my brain to my heart, encompassing, collecting, and disposing of any and all things negative, and leaving in their place three fledgling seeds of change: *benevolence, patience,* and *understanding.* I hope that those seeds of change will take root and grow into ideals to live by. It won't be easy, but anything worth having takes hard work and sacrifice. I consider benevolence, patience, and understanding to be disciplines that need to be worked on every moment of every day if they are to become involuntary, subconscious ways of life. So now, instead of dreading having to drive, I look at driving as the practice field where I can hone my skills in those important ethoses.

INDEX

Rondre Summerville

AUTHOR BIO

C.D. Rencher was born in Centerville, Illinois. He grew up in E. St. Louis, Illinois. After graduating from high school, he served 11 years honorably in the United States Air Force (5 years active duty, 6 years active reserves). In 1995, he began his career in the bar business, over the course of the last 17 years he has held for the most part every position in the Hospitality Service Industry(doorman, server, bartender, Disc Jockey, bar and restaurant manager, Beverage Manager). The last 4 years his primary occupation has been working as the dayshift bartender at a hotel, downtown St. Louis.

CPSIA information can be obtained at www.ICGtesting.com
Printed in the USA
LVOW041426100812

293833LV00001B/52/P